CW00433268

Poems for the Beekeeper

Poems for the Beekeeper

Edited by Robert Gent

Five Leaves Publications

Poems for the Beekeeper

Published in 1996 by Five Leaves Publications
PO Box 81, Nottingham NG5 4ER

Published with financial assistance from

EAST
MIDLANDS
ARTS

and the support of Nottinghamshire County Council

Collection copyright: Five Leaves Publications
Copyright for individual poems rests with the authors

The Beekeeper statue by Sioban Coppinger
Cover photograph by Patrick Henry
Design by 4 Sheets
Printed in Great Britain by Antony Rowe

ISBN 0 907123 82 1

CONTENTS

***Dannie Abse** is a doctor who was born in Cardiff in 1923. His first collection of poetry was published in 1948 and since then he has published numerous books of poetry and autobiography. The poems reproduced below are taken from **On the Evening Road**, published by Hutchinson in 1994.*

The Mistake

Come this way through the wooden gate into our garden.
Confront the green tree which once had no identity.
Pluck a leaf. Close your eyes. Smell its acrid odour.
Does it suggest an Oriental dispensary?

One day (after thirteen years) a tree-expert told us
its name: '*Evodia danieli*, without doubt.
From Korea. Odd to find it thriving here in Wales.'
We thanked him. Now we had something to boast about.

When visitors came we offered them a leaf proudly.
'Breathe this in,' we'd urge. 'It's rare as Welsh gold.'
Our olfactory gift, our pagan benediction.
'From Korea,' we'd swank. 'It'll charm away your cold.'

Who, in all of Great Britain, possessed such treasure?
But then came the summer of the drought. Tired of lies
the parched tree suddenly asserted itself, sprouted
ordinary walnuts, shamelessly free of disguise.

Breakfast Together

She sits opposite me
the other side of the breakfast table,
doesn't know that last week
I murdered her.

Oh pure, flawless love!
It would have altered — leaves are falling now —
with the passing years.

Consider the statistics of divorce.
The possible prolegomenon:
secret phone-calls,
furtive appointments,
marital violence even.

Man, man, never strike a woman
for if you do
she'll have dominion
over you.

No, no not that. None of that
as the leaves fall, the passing years.

So I arranged her funeral,
no expense spared —
a secular funeral; a hush of black cars;
flowers galore, a veritable park!

The mortician's arms folded, head bowed.

I thought of playing that tape,
that Beethoven *Cavatina*,
that anguished music she loved best,
music so remote, so terrible.

Instead I chose the old dance-tune
my mother-in-law liked:
'Stay as sweet as you are,
don't let a thing ever change you.'
Appropriate, *n'est-ce-pas?*

Afterwards, the wake that I had planned.
A joyous feast! Drinks galore!
We had everything except balloons.

And there she is now, not knowing any of this,
sitting the other side of the table,
alluring still, spooning a grapefruit,
mirthless, reading the *Guardian* —
she, only one week less perfect.

Two Photographs

Here's a photograph of grandmother, Annabella.
How slim she appears, how vulnerable. Pretty.
And here's a photograph of grandmother, Doris.
How portly she looks, formidable. Handsome.
Annabella wears a demure black frock with an amber brooch.
Doris, a lacy black gown with a string of pearls.
One photo's marked *Ystalfera* 1880,
the other *Bridgend* 1890.
Both were told to say, 'Cheese'; one, defiant, said 'Chalk!'

Annabella spoke Welsh with a Patagonian accent.
Doris spoke English with a Welsh Valleys' lilt.
Annabella fasted — pious, passive, enjoyed small-talk.
Doris feasted — pacy, pushy, would never pray. Ate pork!
When Annabella told Doris she was damned
indecorous Doris devilishly laughed.
I liked Doris, I liked Annabella,
though Doris was bossy and Annabella daft.
I do not think they liked each other.

Last night I dreamed they stood back to back,
not for the commencement of a duel
but to see who was taller! Now, in these revived
waking hours, my Eau de Cologne grandmothers
with buns of grey hair, of withered rose,
seem illusory, fugitive, like my dream -
or like the dust that secretively flows
in a sudden sunbeam (sieved through leaky curtains)
and disappears when and where that sunbeam goes.

Of two old ladies once uxoriously loved,
what's survived? An amber brooch, a string of pearls,
two photographs. Happening on them, my children's
grandchildren will ask 'Who?' — hardly aware
that if this be not true, I never lived.

Fleur Adcock *was born in New Zealand but has spent two thirds of her life in England. Her most recent collections of poems are* **The Incident Book** *and* **Time-Zones**, *both published by Oxford University Press.*

Post Office

The queue's right out through the glass doors
to the street: Thursday, pension day.
They built this Post Office too small.
Of course, the previous one was smaller —
a tiny prefab, next to the betting-shop,
says the man who's just arrived;
and the present one, at which we're queuing,
was cherry-trees in front of a church.
The church was where the supermarket is:
'My wife and I got married in that church'
the man says. 'We hold hands sometimes
when we're standing waiting at the check-out —
have a little moment together!' He laughs.
The queue shuffles forward a step.
Three members of it silently vow
never to grow old in this suburb;
one vows never to grow old at all.
'I first met her over there' the man says,
'on that corner where the bank is now.
The other corner was Williams Brothers —
remember Williams Brothers? They gave you tokens,
tin money, like, for your dividend.'
The woman in front of him remembers.
She nods, and swivels her loose lower denture,
remembering Williams Brothers' metal tokens,
and the marble slab on the cheese-counter,

9

and the carved mahogany booth where you went to pay.
The boy in front of her is chewing gum;
his jaws rotate with the same motion
as hers: to and fro, to and fro.

For Heidi with Blue Hair

When you dyed your hair blue
(or, at least, ultramarine
for the clipped sides, with a crest
of jet-black spikes on top)
you were sent home from school

because, as the headmistress put it,
although dyed hair was not
specifically forbidden, yours
was, apart from anything else,
not done in the school colours.

Tears in the kitchen, telephone-calls
to school from your freedom-loving father:
'She's not a punk in her behaviour;
it's just a style.' (You wiped your eyes,
also not in a school colour.)

'She discussed it with me first —
we checked the rules.' 'And anyway, Dad,
it cost twenty-five dollars.
Tell them it won't wash out —
not even if I wanted to try.'

It would have been unfair to mention
your mother's death, but that
shimmered behind the arguments.
The school had nothing else against you;
the teachers twittered and gave in.

Next day your black friend had hers done
in grey, white and flaxen yellow —
the school colours precisely:
an act of solidarity, a witty
tease. The battle was already won.

James Berry has published books of poetry with New Beacon and OUP. His stories and poems for children are published in the UK and USA. The following poems are taken from an extensive new collection of poems for adults — **Hot Earth Cold Earth** — which was published by Bloodaxe Books in July 1995.

Faces Around My Father

Hunger stormed my arrival.
I arrived needing.
I had need of older selves.
My mother's milk met
my parching. Streams were here
like stars and stones,
and a fatherhood compelling.

Fatherhood tailed a line
of fathers, we knew: a prehistory
book, a full season open all time,
a storehouse for emptying
for renewal, a marketing
of strength that stuffs away
richness of summers upon summers.

I'd work up a clean slate full.
Crafts and arts would engage me,
my urgent hands would grow
in homely voices,
the land would amaze
my roaming eyes,
incite my impulses.

Head striped, sir, with sounds
of birds in the hills,
sweat smells in clothes stuck
with soil and sun, you come
into the house at evening
like a piece of hillside.
I wait to take your drinking mug.

A silence surrounds your eating.
The dog catches and gulps
pieces of food you pitch
that somehow cut your distance.
A son washes your feet.
Another brings glowing firewood:
you light up your pipe.

Your incidental money getting
not believed, a child asks for cash
for boots or book.
Our words are stones
tossed on a genial guest.
You vanish into twilight.
A sleeping house receives you back.

And father is a scripture
lesson. Father knows
blueprints of seeds in the moon,
knows place of a cockerel's
testicles, knows coins
in minutes. His body sets
defences, sets boundaries.

Yet strong hints had soaked us:
we are not beautiful,
we are a cancellation
of abundance and sharing.
I am charged with unmanageable
hunger. I am trumpeted
for ungettable distances.

I must cross our moat of sea,
and I have no way. I must list
lost tracks, must write
my scanning of time, must plant
hot words in ministers like cool
communion bread. Yet I should drown
in language of our lanes.

In and about your preclusion, sir,
dead footsteps entrapped me.
You chopped wood and sang,
I listened behind a wall.
In hot field of pineapples
fermenting, I watched you
dreaming: I walked away.

Your tool's edge touched work
barely, and you resharpened.
Sir, in fresh sunny magnitude,
your dramatic grind of machete
should flatten forests. Yet
you left for work looking,
'What boss shall I serve today?'

Were you being your father
or just a loser's son? Sir,
did old scars warn you to yield
and hide? Were you strangely
full of a friendly enemy
voice? Did you feel
your movements failure-fixed?

Schemed in your steady
good health, we were placed
to proliferate loneliness,
birthdays of lacks,
trouble growing in our flesh,
lips moved by ventriloquists,
beginnings with approaches of daggers.

We needed that safety, sir,
that wonderment of caressing eye,
that steadiness that allows
strongest and sweetest voice,
that sanctioned contentment
that walked bright
in the constellation of children.

Our voices deepened,
our limbs emulated trees,
our appetites expanded,
our silence encircled you
like strangers with killer plans.
I disowned you to come to know
thanks to connection that someone may feel.

I saw your body full
and fit and free, ready
in the sun's recycle,
ever the husbandman
of exalted exclamations.
I saw you die, sir,
well bluffed by subjugation.

Spirits of Movement

Surely, so alike, airborne wind gave birth
to water, issued the denser wash
and earthed the early offspring.

Inbuilt is wind-inheritance.
Rage of leaves resists face-wash
it is wind's arrival in trees.

Hear sea waves work-choir,
hear any waterfall wonder,
its temple-roar of wind flooding woods.

A restless transparent busyness
going and going. Spirits of movement.
Both break all shores, mad mad in search.

Wind plays wild bands of ghosts.
Water organises running river
and drives rain-floods hustling.

On any sitting duty
like being a pond or puddle
canal or glassful

water waits to run away
or just disappear like wind.
In a settled state water is sad.

Drop a stone in a sleepy pool
you hear the sulk
of static water voiced.

Lock up water, give it time, it'll leave.
Drink it down, it presses wanting exit.
A job done, water vanishes.

Water'll freshen any body part
and be ready, hanging
in drips, to be off.

Does its work, yes. But to be
ungraspable, like wind,
water insists on its transfiguration.

Alan Brownjohn's nine volumes of poetry include **The Observation Car**, 1990 and **In the Cruel Arcade**, 1994. *The seven previous volumes are represented in his* **Collected Poems**, *1988. He is also the author of two novels,* **The Way You Tell Them** *(winner of the Authors' Club prize for the most promising first novel of 1990) and* **The Long Shadows**, *published in 1996 in Romanian.*

Profoundest Love

She gave him sand from the Tyrrhenian Sea,
He sent her a present of sand from the shores of Lake Erie.

He dropped some grains of her sand on the edge of the lake,
But kept the others, it helped him remember her.
She mingled a bit of his sand with the verge of the sea,
But retained some grains in a tiny box because
They reminded her of him.

And this was happening everywhere in the world,
Whole deserts exchanged between Asia and Africa,
And people everywhere swopping seedlings and saplings,
Whole forests exchanged between Finland and Brazil.

Cat-lovers transplanted whiskers from their cats:
'My cat has your cat's whisker and yours mine.'
We think of each other much more often that way.

I stood by the motorway watching the sand trucks pass,
I saw huge lorries transporting uprooted trees,
I saw vets' ambulances speeding with mad blue lights
— The whiskers for the transplants.

My name is Vladimir Nikolaich:
Back indoors I switch on a radio I cannot understand,
I am in High Wycombe, the news is English here.
My Rosemary knows no Russian, I love her so much,
And she is in Kharkov switching on the radio
And comprehending nothing in the least

— Except that we exchanged for one another,
And think of each other very much indeed.
Ours was an act of the profoundest love.

Lieder

(For Peter Porter)

Horseman, horseman galloping with the wind! Look at me, look
at me, I am the beautiful daughter of the King of the Hobgoblins. If
you look at me but once I will gallop at your side, and lead you
down, down, into the caverns of the Hobgoblins.

The poet sings: Although I am forbidden your company, although
you write me whole pages, whole books, whole libraries of cruel
rejection, I shall still come and play my piccolo under your casement.
Remember, only timid young ladies obey their mothers.

The young man says: You may think I am like a kite on your
string, that I will obey every tug of your heartless fingers. Beware,
beware! One day I shall refuse your bidding and flop down into the
mud.

The poet sings: I love my cat, and I love you. My cat is small and
warm, and so are you. My cat plays with me and has sharp claws,
and so do you.

The young peasant is very lazy, but his beloved is very short in
stature. I will take up my shears, he says, and cut and cut at the grass
until I can see you, my dear. What wonders, O what wonders love
will accomplish!

She says: If you are a butterfly, I shall be a net. If you are a rose, I
shall be a pair of secateurs. If you are some crisps, I shall be a
wrapper, and you will be ready salted. I am a most determined
young woman.

The poet, starving and penniless, sings for the King. O what gifts,
O what glories, says the King. They are worth more than all the
banquets and all the gold in the world — and turns the poet out into
the snow at the palace gate.

Looking at Her

When he looked at her, he invariably felt
Like stretching his arms up, as if about to do
A long and lustrous yawn. Of course she knew
She had that effect; and whether she lounged or knelt,
Or walked or simply stood, he was never clear
If she was prepared and eager to let him bring
His hands down around her neck, and press her near
— Or would shake her head and permit him no such thing.

This was her talent, to stir both lust and doubt,
She did it best of all feats she was able;
And therefore other women felt sure she bored
The men she attracted; since all of them, without
Her seeming to provoke them, of one accord
Would yawn and thump their fists down on the table.

Catherine Byron grew up in Belfast and has lived in Scotland and England since leaving Ireland. She now lives in Leicester. Her most recent books are the semi-autobiographical **Out of Step: Pursuing Seamus Heaney to Purgatory** and the poetry collection **The Fat-Hen Field Hospital**

SILK AND BELFAST LINEN

I. The Lampshade Makers

First, a slow and ravelled bandaging
of wire, the soldered junctions awkward,
the frame a snare for their wrists,
and that flat card of cross-cut binding
a footling shuttle as they lay the tape's
raw edge round ferrous metal
that would else, in this sporey climate, oxidise.

And then they take their trousseaux
all to bits — all their night things
snip-snipped to a panel pattern:
the camisoles and wedding negligees
of silk and silk-satin and silk-mousseline.
They cut away chafed seams, stained underarms,
faint foxing of blood below.

Oh, there are stretches that are good
as new, blush pink and peachy!
These they seam into a sleeve of silk
and raise a taut pavilion.
                                   Now
silk's in eclipse until its lamp is lit.

22

II. Shears

In the linen mills I was a weaver of linen.
(That was before I married Billy Morrow.)
My own loom, uh huh, my own web.
Them was great times. Forty of us girls
pedalling Belfast linen on forty looms.

But yer man — Robinson, was it? — would saunter along
the aisle of the looms. Didn't he have the quick eye
for a slub in the damask, even a thickened thread.
He had soft hands. The other checkers'd point
so as you could mend it. Robinson? Oh no.

His wee white nail'd
pick and pick and pick
till that slub was a hole in the web
and the pink prick of his finger
poked right through.

'Yon's a fault!' Robinson dandered his shears
handy like, at his belt. In four snips
he'd cut the warp in two. 'That'll larn ye.'

Mebbe a day's piece gone. Mebbe a week's.
Whatever it was, it was a ruin of linen.
Priceless. The girl wageless. And in debt for the yarn.

Wendy Cope *was born in Erith, Kent. She was educated at Farrington's School and subsequently went to St. Hilda's College, Oxford, where she learned to play the guitar. After university she worked for fifteen years as a primary-school teacher in London. In 1987 she received a Cholmondeley Award for poetry. Her published collections for adults include* **Making Cocoa for Kingsley Amis** *(1986),* **Serious Concerns** *(1992) and* **The River Girl***, (1991), all published by Faber and Faber.*

Some More Light Verse

You have to try. You see a shrink.
You learn a lot. You read. You think.
You struggle to improve your looks.
You meet some men. You write some books.
You eat good food. You give up junk.
You do not smoke. You don't get drunk.
You take up yoga, walk and swim.
And nothing works. The outlook's grim.
You don't know what to do. You cry.
You're running out of things to try.

You blow your nose. You see the shrink.
You walk. You give up food and drink.
You fall in love. You make a plan.
You struggle to improve your man.
And nothing works. The outlook's grim.
You go to yoga, cry and swim.
You eat and drink. You give up looks.
You struggle to improve your books.
You cannot see the point. You sigh.
You do not smoke. You have to try.

Before she cries out, I gather her up,
still surprised at the lightness, the bird-like
vulnerability of her warm soft body.
She breathes, and breathes and breathes
like a mantra for new mornings.

(for Akua)

Oakland Avenue

Oakland Avenue reads like a scripture,
a chronicle of the past, the changing dispensations.
Here the dead speak beyond the grave,
through the warped insecurities of the living,
trying to sustain some orderliness in heaven and hell.
Their resting places, separate houses, divided
by Sumtonian lines of decency.
The Jewish bones feed from below the tangle
of jasmine vines, the flowers of lamentation;
the Catholics wait for the trump to sound
that they may rise and walk the ladder to glory,
shattering the lovingly wrought tombstones in the green;
the white Baptists rest in Abraham's bosom,
where the lines are clearly drawn — ne'er the twain shall
meet;
and in the unruly corner under the dark of live oaks
rest the Black Baptists, Black Catholics, Black Jews and
all.
For the optimistic, this is a vision of the splendour
of eternity, the accommodation of the dead to neighbours;
separately equal in the waiting time — there is order
here.
But I, walking this avenue late at night,
smelling the fresh of healthy vegetation,
have imagined the sound of the crazy trumpet,

29

imagined the sky flaming with blood red,
the cracking of the old concrete slabs, the handclaps
 of the trees stirred by a hot dry wind;
I have imagined what the waiting line will be like:
 separate lines, despite the pallid sameness
of the worm-cleaned bones, the same dank stench
 of the risen dead? Will the eyes
still be averted, not making four, will there be songs
 for all to sing; or is the new robe of resurrection
a garment so complete that all we have thought we are
 will be but a reflection, a pale imitation?
This is eternal. I reflect, here in this place
 of multiple fences. Even in death, even in death
our imaginations remain hemmed by a lie.
 Hasten your coming, Saviour, that the question
may be answered clear as new day;
 for our eyes can see little beyond the temporal
and what a miserable condition it is, what a miserable
thing.

Some Tentative Definitions XI

"Every time I hear the sound of the whip..."

For every chekeh of the guitar,
a whip cracks,
how can you hear the sound
and not weep?

Follow the pattern with me,
always on the off.
We are forever searching for spaces
to fill with us.

If you walk straight down on the one
you will stumble
cause the reggae walk is a bop
to the off beat.

We are always finding spaces
in the old scores
to build our homes, temples and dreams
and we call it back-o-wall.

For every *wooku* of the hammond B
a body hums.
How can you smell the sound
and still sleep?

*Carol Ann Duffy was born in Glasgow and brought up in Staffordshire. Her first three collections, **Standing Female Nude, The Other Country** and **Selling Manhattan**, brought her critical acclaim and numerous awards. **Mean Time**, published in 1993 by Anvil Press, won a Scottish Arts Council Book Award, the 1993 Whitbread Award for poetry and the Forward Prize.*

Litany

The soundtrack then was a litany — *candlewick
bedspread three piece suite display cabinet —*
and stiff-haired wives balanced their red smiles,
passing the catalogue. *Pyrex.* A tiny ladder
ran up Mrs Barr's American Tan leg, sly
like a rumour. Language embarrassed them.

The terrible marriages crackled, cellophane
round polyester shirts, and then The Lounge
would seem to bristle with eyes, hard
as the bright stones in engagement rings,
and sharp hands poised over biscuits as a word
was spelled out. An embarrassing word, broken

to bits, which tensed the air like an accident.
This was the code I learnt at my mother's knee,
 pretending
to read, where no one had cancer, or sex, or debts,
and certainly not leukaemia, which no one could
 spell.
The year a mass grave of wasps bobbed in a jam-jar;
a butterfly stammered itself in my curious hands.

A boy in the playground, I said, *told me*
to fuck off; and a thrilled, malicious pause
salted my tongue like an imminent storm. Then
uproar. *I'm sorry, Mrs Barr, Mrs Hunt, Mrs Emery,*
sorry, Mrs Raine. Yes, I can summon their names.
My mother's mute shame. The taste of soap.

Warming Her Pearls
for Judith Radstone

Next to my own skin, her pearls. My mistress
bids me wear them, warm them, until evening
when I'll brush her hair. At six, I place them
round her cool, white throat. All day I think of her,

resting in the Yellow Room, contemplating silk
or taffeta, which gown tonight? She fans herself
whilst I work willingly, my slow heat entering
each pearl. Slack on my neck, her rope.

She's beautiful. I dream about her
in my attic bed; picture her dancing
with tall men, puzzled by my faint, persistent scent
beneath her French perfume, her milky stones.

I dust her shoulders with a rabbit's foot,
watch the soft blush seep through her skin
like an indolent sigh. In her looking-glass
my red lips part as though I want to speak.

Full moon. Her carriage brings her home. I see
her every movement in my head...Undressing,
taking off her jewels, her slim hand reaching
for the case, slipping naked into bed, the way

33

she always does...And I lie here awake,
knowing the pearls are cooling even now
in the room where my mistress sleeps. All night
I feel their absence and I burn.

Mrs Aesop

By Christ, he could bore for Purgatory. He was small,
didn't prepossess. So he tried to impress. *Dead men,*
Mrs Aesop, he'd say, *tell no tales.* Well, let me tell you
  now
that the bird in his hand shat on his sleeve,
never mind the two worth less in the bush. Tedious.

Going out was worst. He'd stand at our gate, look,
  then leap;
scour the hedgerows for a shy mouse, the fields
for a sly fox, the sky for one particular swallow
  that couldn't make a summer. The jackdaw, according
  to him,
envied the eagle. Donkeys would, on the whole, prefer
  to be lions.

On one appalling evening stroll, we passed an old hare
snoozing in a ditch — he stopped and made a note —
and then, about a mile further on, a tortoise, somebody's
  pet
creeping, slow as marriage, up the road. *Slow*
but certain, Mrs Aesop, wins the race. Asshole.

What race? What sour grapes? What silk purse,
sow's ear, dog in a manger, what big fish? Some days,
I could barely keep awake as the story droned on
towards the moral of itself. *Action, Mrs A., speaks louder*
than words. And that's another thing, the sex

was diabolical. I gave him a fable one night
about a little cock that wouldn't crow, a razor-sharp axe
with a heart blacker than the pot that called the kettle.
I'll cut off your tail, all right, I said, *to save my face.*
That shut him up. I laughed last, longest.

Helen Dunmore is a poet and novelist. *The poems printed here are taken from her collection for children,* **Secrets**, *which won the 1995 Signal Poetry Award.*

Breeze of Ghosts

Tall ship hanging out at the horizon
tall ship blistering the horizon
you've been there so long
your sheets and decks white
in the sun

what wind whispers you in?

Tall ship creaking at the horizon
your captain long gone
your crew in the cabin
drinking white rum
their breath spiralling

what wind breathes you in?

Tall ship tilting to the shoreline
past Spanish palms
tall ship coming in like a swan
in the midday sun

what wind blows you in?

It is the cool
wind of the morning
stirring my masts
before the sun
burns it to nothing,
they call it
breeze of ghosts.

Yellow

Think of something yellow.

The sun?
A fat ripe pear
or buttercup petals?

Yellow is butter.
Yellow is custard.
Yellow is yolks.

Yellow has all the answers.
Yellow is like
an advert that twists your eyes
till they light on yellow.

What is yellow?

Nobody answered.
Shakeela smiled
and stroked her yellow
shalwar khameez
so butterly
and buttercuply
that all our fingers turned yellow.

Night Cat

She's there by the fence
but you mustn't call out,
like a scoop of night
or a water shadow
tense for flight
she'll twist and go,
don't open your mouth —
the moon's so close
that the stars blow out —
you turn she's gone
leaving that patch
where the moon shone
leaving the empty
dress of night
with the stars picked out
and you alone.

Gavin Ewart, *who died in 1995, was one of the wittiest and most memorable poets of his generation. His entertaining and wryly-observed verse — often very short — was deceptive in its simplicity. Gavin Ewart's technical mastery enabled him to pack a serious message into what appeared to be an effortlessly humorous poem.*

The Young Pobble's Guide to his Toes

Everything comes, everything goes.
Some day you must say goodbye to your toes —
all bitten off by the beasts of the sea
or fading away by a gradual degree,
vanishing into an elbowless night
all blurred and dim in your elderly sight.
The sun goes down and the eyes give up,
your toes will fade, kerflip, kerflup...

The moral shines bright as a mermaid's hair.
Count them and keep them while they're still there!

Haiku: A Japanese Dried Flower at a Poetry Reading

Take a poet. Drop
him in alcohol. He'll ex-
pand in full colour!

In the Old People's Home (1914)

This is the last anchorage. HMS *Incontinent*
is in trouble and signals of distress
come from HMS *Repetitive* and HMS *Wanderer*.
HMS *Anxiety* is getting steam up.
The harbour is full of signs of activity,
which are all ignored by HMS *Vainglorious*
as she rides at anchor in perpetual majesty.

Across the water, puffing busily,
come the officious tugs *Snapper* and *Orderly*.

In Memoriam Sir John Betjeman

So the last date slides into the bracket
that will appear in all future anthologies —
and in quiet Cornwall and in London's ghastly racket
we are now Betjemanless.
Your verse was very fetching
and, as Byron might have written,
there are many poetic personalities around
that would fetch a man less!

Some of your admirers were verging on the stupid,
you were envied by poets (more highbrow, more
inventive?);
at twenty you had the bow-shaped lips of a Cupid
(a scuffle with Auden too).
But long before your Oxford
and the visiting of churches
you went topographical — on the Underground
(Metroland and Morden too)!

The Dragon School — but Marlborough a real dragon,
with real bullying, followed the bear of childhood,
a kind of gentlemanly cross to crucify a fag on.
We don't repent at leisure,
you were good, and very British.
Serious, considered 'funny',
in your best poems, strong but sad, we found
a most terrific pleasure.

Reputations

Poets are very touchy. They have to be the greatest.
Or (if not quite *that*) at least the latest.

*U.A. **Fanthorpe*** *has written six books of poems, has three times been a writer in residence, has been a set text for three Examination Boards, and is published by Peterloo Poets and Penguin.*

Awkward Subject

The light is wonderful, he says. Not light
For house-agents, certainly. They avoid
November shots, when wisped and bony trees
Throw a disturbing shade on property.

Stand there. Just a bit further. Don't look at the dog.
My casual adaptation to the place
(One hand in pocket, right knee slightly bent)
May not be what I mean, but is in danger
Of immortality.

     I feel my teeth support me
Against my inner lip; face him with all my skin.
Sensing my misery, *Would you rather smile?*
He asks. And break the lens, I hope. Words are my element.
Photograph them.

Dying Fall

November's leaves flock ginger and stiff along the gutter,
Waiting for the wind to say.

Boots (black), shoes (brown), knee-socks (white).
Their feet speak for them:

Brownies and cubs (eyes left to grin at Mum),
WRVS, swinging arms whose baskets we know,

Guides, Scouts, Sea Scouts, all different, all tweaked
Into step by the bully band,

And the band's irresistible, dammit. I choose not to conform,
I don't want to fight, but by jingo jingo jingo ...

Thin irregular pipe of peace, please. Not this rude
Heartbeat that fuses us all

With the bowler-hatted grey shufflers and their hulking flag,
Grasped cack-handed in a gauntlet,

And the washed dim names that no-one remembers,
Who died in a muddle of bugle-calls

And the fitful drumbeat of glory,
Ending up, like leaves, in mud,

Skulls, tongueless bells, miming their message,
Waiting for the wind to say.

Elaine Feinstein was born in Leicester and in 1990 received an Honorary D.Lit from Leicester University. She has published over thirty books, including fiction and biography, and has written for radio and television. She was made a Fellow of the Royal Society of Literature in 1980 and received a Cholmondeley Award in 1990.

Dad

Your old hat hurts me, and those black
 fat raisins you liked to press into
my palm from your soft heavy hand.
 I see you staggering back up the path
with sacks of potatoes from some local farm,
 fresh eggs, flowers. Every day I grieve

for your great heart broken and you gone.
 You loved to watch the trees. This year
you did not see their Spring.
 The sky was freezing over the fen
as on that somewhere secretly appointed day
 you beached: cold, white-faced, shivering.

What happened, old bull, my loyal
 hoarse-voiced warrior? The hammer
blow that stopped you in your track
 and brought you to a hospital monitor
could not destroy your courage
 to the end you were
uncowed and unconcerned with pleasing anyone.

I think of you now as once again safely
 at my mother's side, the earth as
chosen as a bed, and feel most sorrow for
 all that was gentle in
my childhood buried there
 already forfeit, now forever lost.

Anniversary

Suppose I took out a slender ketch from
under the spokes of Palace pier tonight to
catch a sea going fish for you

or dressed in antique goggles and wings and
flew down through sycamore leaves into the park

or luminescent through some planetary strike
put one delicate flamingo leg over the sill of your lab

Could I surprise you? or would you insist on
keeping a pattern to link every transfiguration?

Listen, I shall have to whisper it
into your heart directly: we are all
supernatural every day
we rise new creatures cannot be predicted

Getting Older

The first surprise: I like it.
Whatever happens now, some things
that used to terrify have not:

I didn't die young, for instance. Or lose
my only love. My three children
never had to run away from anyone.

Don't tell me this gratitude is complacent.
We all approach the edge of the same blackness
which for me is silent.

Knowing as much sharpens
my delight in January freesia,
hot coffee, winter sunlight. So we say

as we lie close on some gentle occasion:
every day won from such
darkness is a celebration.

John Harvey *is author of the Nottingham-based Charlie Resnick crime novels, publisher of Slow Dancer Press, scriptwriter and poet.*

Seven Year Ache

"There's nothing so spiritual about being happy
but you can't miss a day of it, beacuse it doesn't last."
Frank O'Hara: Poem (And tomorrow morning at 8 o'clock)

Listlessly listening to the radio this afternoon,
those brittle repetitions of Glass, the London
brick and tile outside scored through by rain,
and as I thumb my well-worn life of Frank O'Hara,
replete with pink and purple annotations,
I chance to notice *Top Hat* is playing on TV
in time to see Fred and Ginger shelter in that so
convenient bandstand and marvel at the grudging way
she mimics him, step by step, through his routine.

And I think of the young Francis watching them
for the first time from those red velvet seats
of the Worcester Warner's with his aunt.
How he loved them! Ginger's 'pageboy bob,'
Fred's 'peach melba voice,' and how, watching
them now, I hate Astaire's smugness, the dinner-
suited certainty with which he knows he will get
the girl, unfailingly, at the end.

Last night, and then again today, I am taunted
by the bizarre easiness of dying; O'Hara at forty
knocked over by an errant jeep upon the beach,
his mother, frail from hospital and drying-out,
tumbling yellow roses into his grave. Such waste!
But take away the orations and the tears, is this
so bad? How many of us would not rather have died
at the height of our powers, five years ago or ten,
taken the same short telling step his friend Berryman
made from that Minnesota bridge?

Each day that's lived is lived in hope and in regret.
We die each day and not from love but lack of it;
the pull of your hand away from mine, the turn
of your face aside. Whatever flowers you hurl
at that fresh-turned earth will carry with them,
bright and unremarkable, the stench of what was missed.

You Did It! You Did It!

"It was Roland Kirk, wasn't it?
Who played all those instruments?
I saw him. St. Pancras Town Hall.
Nineteen sixty four."

The same year, in the old Marquee,
not long out of college, cock-sure,
I saw Henry 'Red' Allen, face swollen like sad fruit,
sing 'I've got the World on a String' in a high
almost falsetto moan that told the truth
beneath the words' exuberant tone
and married you — desperate to dull the ache
I thought simply came from being alone.

Eight years of slow denial later, faith
and tempers frayed, both at the end
of our respective rope, we broke,
raw and gaping, back into the world, intent
on reinventing our lives, sick with need
as new-born mice, pink-eyed,
snuffling blind mouths against unseen teets;
greedy for life as Rahsaan Roland Kirk,
on stage in this cold country, nineteen sixty four,
cramming his mouth with saxophones, harmonica,
reed trumpet, piccolo and clarinet,
exultant, black and blind, the whoop and siren call
of flutes and whistles, spiralling music unconfined.

You did it! You did it!
You did it! You did it!

Daring us to turn our backs,
stop off our hearts and ears,
deny the blood wherever it leads us:
fail.

Self Portrait

Bonnard at Le Cannet

Cold here, this room you sit in, 1945,
your small corner table,
vase of flowers and white cloth,
grey scarf pulled close about your neck,
the light that collects like pennies in your eyes.
Still, you sit and smoke, patient for cognac,
warm in its glass, the small black coffee,
its white cup with gold rim which she will bring,
except for three years she has not appeared at your call.

Like an otter, sleek, she would ease from the bath,
again and again in all the pages of this diary,
Saturday, February 26th, Tuesday the 15th of June,
and here she lies immersed in water,
snug against the curve of porcelain.

You sit and stare. The air is rimed with smoke
and the far echo of guns.
On the radio this morning, news of the Armistice,
the hastily articulated peace, the Jews.
A newspaper open on the long wooden table,
shrouded in grey cloth.
The small electric heater stands unplugged,
no fire in the grate and still the smell of smoke.
Each of these last mornings you have walked down
between the olive, orange and almond trees,
gazed over red roofs towards the fullness of the sea.
You have painted ochres, orange-reds and browns,
cupboards steeped in coloured jars and bottles,
herbs in bunches, greengages and plums,
golden apples, persimmons.

What were you looking for?

In the studio the slow shunt of trucks,
smell of paint thick between your fingers.
Stiff-legged before the mirror, scarf
well tucked down, you blow warmth
into your hands. Head shaved, ready,
this is not so difficult, this portrait.
A gash of colour for the mouth,
those veins, blue, drawn down across
the fabric of the face, black hollows
where the eyes would once have been,
burnt out by bodies that hang ripening
and lay, close-pressed, between the trees,
their richness leaking back into the soil,
or float there, out of reach of seeing,
stripped beneath the surface of the sea.

Adrian Henri *was born Birkenhead in 1932. Hons.BA Fine Art 1955. Fairground-worker, scenic artist and schoolteacher 1955-61. Manchester then Liverpool Colleges of Art 1961-68. Led poetry/rock group Liverpool Scene 1967-70. Since then freelance painter and poet, art critic, performer and occasional playwright and songwriter. Honorary D.Litt. Liverpool 1990.*
Poetry: **Not Fade Away** *1994;* **Wish You Were Here** *1990;* **Collected Poems** *1986. Poetry for children:* **Dinner With the Spratts** *1993;* **Box** *1990;* **Rhinestone Rhino** *1989;* **The Phantom Lollipop Lady** *1986. Playscript:* **The Wakefield Mysteries** *1991.*

Any Prince to Any Princess

August is coming
and the goose, I'm afraid,
is getting fat.
There have been
no golden eggs for some months now.
Straw has fallen well below market price
despite my frantic spinning
and the sedge is,
as you rightly point out,
withered.

I can't imagine how the pea
got under your mattress. I apologize
humbly. The chambermaid has, of course,
been sacked. As has the frog footman.
I understand that, during my recent fact-finding tour of the
 Golden River,
despite your nightly unavailing efforts,
he remained obstinately
froggish.

51

I hope that the three wishes granted by the General
  Assembly
will go some way towards redressing
this unfortunate recent sequence of events.
The fall in output from the shoe-factory, for example:
no one could have foreseen the work-to-rule
by the National Union of Elves. Not to mention the fact
that the court has been fast asleep
for the last six and a half years.
The matter of the poisoned apple has been taken up
by the Board of Trade: I think I can assure you
the incident will not be repeated.

I can quite understand, in the circumstances,
your reluctance to let down
your golden tresses. However
I feel I must point out
that the weather isn't getting any better
and I already have a nasty chill
from waiting at the base
of the White Tower. You must see
the absurdity of the situation.
Some of the courtiers are beginning to talk,
not to mention the humble villagers.
It's been three weeks now, and not even a word.

Princess,
a cold, black wind
howls through our empty palace.
Dead leaves litter the bedchamber;
the mirror on the wall hasn't said a thing
since you left. I can only ask,
bearing all this in mind,
that you think again,

let down your hair,

reconsider.

The Bell

The bell
tolled all afternoon
we did not send to ask
for whom.
It told of flowers
heaped in a goalmouth,
red and blue scarves
heaped together at an altar;
it told of
eyes like T.V. screens
haunted by last night's images,
tears dried by the April wind.
As the flags at half-mast
stirred overhead
the deep bell
still tolled in our heads
long after the light had gone.

Love in Blackpool

In a famous seaside place
that's noted for fresh air and not much else tonight,
the lights from The Tower are lost in the fog;
a lone dog patrols the shrouded beach;
ghosts of pink, cheeky-bottomed girls,
huge striped men who can't see their little Willy
haunt the deserted Pier,
The Winter Gardens.
In every shuttered gift shop window
dusty sticks with horses-head handles;
faded bars of rock
lettered all through, say
I LOVE YOU. The bitter wind
has fish-and-chips on its breath.

Selima Hill *is an internationally-known writer, tutor and reader of her work, whose awards include the Cholmondeley Award for Literature, an Arts Council Writer's Bursary and UEA Writing Fellowship. Her sixth collection,* **Violet**, *was published by Bloodaxe in 1996.*

Being Fifty Makes Me Feel Large

Being fifty makes me feel large,
large and cold,
like someone else's fridge.
I harbour scarlet fish
and fat gold eggs
that men in suits
with hands like vets'
remove.
I never speak.

Sometimes I might hum;
or, very rarely,
raise a strangled gurgle,
as if I'm trying one last time to lurch forward,
to get my fluff-clogged ankles
free from the lino,
hone myself, develop a fluked tail,
acquire a taste for frogbit,
and push off —

paddle off across the world's wide oceans
like a flat-footed sofa
that's suddenly learnt how to swim,
piled high with jellies, cheeses, cushions,
fishes, poodles, babies, balding men,
swimming-pools, airing-cupboards, hospitals,
and tiny pills, like polystyrene granules,
people advise one, or not,
to start taking.

Silence

Her path, if you can call it one, is silence,
obviously quite different from our own,
and one, as I have said, that we will monitor.
It's true she makes my people here uneasy —
she makes it hard to go on acting normally,
and not to call in question one's beliefs.
Another thing — her smell of chickenfeed.
To be precise, of chickenfeed and lemon.
Curled up on my eiderdown this morning,
she looked like something put there to annoy me —
and I must admit I felt a strong temptation
to wring her little neck, and dispose of her,
which would have been quite easy in the circumstances,
there being no bright feathers to betray us.

Cow

I want to be a cow
and not my mother's daughter.
I want to be a cow
and not in love with you.
I want to feel free to feel calm.
I want to be a cow who never knows
the kind of love you 'fall in love with' with;
a queenly cow, with hips as big and sound
as a department store,
a cow the farmer milks on bended knee,
who when she dies will feel dawn
bending over her like lawn to wet her lips.

I want to be a cow,
nothing fancy —
a cargo of grass,
a hammock of soupy milk
whose floating and rocking and dribbling's undisturbed
by the echo of hooves to the city;
of crunching boots;
of suspicious-looking trailers parked on verges;
of unscrupulous restaurant-owners
who stumble, pink-eyed, from stale beds
into a world of lobsters and warm telephones;
of streamlined Japanese freighters
ironing the night;
heavy with sweet desire like bowls of jam.

The Tibetans have 85 words for states of consciousness.
This dozy cow I want to be has none.
She doesn't speak.
She doesn't do housework or worry about her appearance.
She doesn't roam.
Safe in her fleet
of shorn-white-bowl-like friends,
she needs, and loves, and's loved by,
only this —
the farm I want to be a cow on too.

Don't come looking for me.
Don't come walking out into the bright sunlight
looking for me,
black in your gloves and stockings and sleeves
and large hat.
Don't call the tractorman.
Don't call the neighbours.
Don't make a special fruit-cake for when I come home:
I'm not coming home.
I'm going to be a cowman's counted cow.
I'm going to be a cow
and you won't know me.

Mick Imlah *was born in Aberdeen in 1956.* **Birthmarks**
(1988) was his first collection; his poems are included in
Penguin Modern Poets 3*; he is currently Poetry Editor
at the Times Literary Supplement.*

Goldilocks

This is a story about the possession of beds.
It begins at the foot of a staircase in Oxford, one midnight,
When (since my flat in the suburbs of London entailed
a fiancee whose claims I did not have the nerve to evict)

I found myself grateful for climbing alone on a spiral
To sleep I could call with assurance exclusively mine,
For there was the name on the oak that the Lodge had assigned
Till the morning to me (how everything tends to its place!)

And flushed with the pleasing (if not unexpected) success
Of the paper on 'Systems of Adult-to-Infant Regression'
With which the Young Fireball had earlier baffled his betters
At the Annual Excuse for Genetics to let down its ringlets,

I'd just sniggered slightly (pushing the unlocked door
Of the room where I thought there was nothing of mine to protect)
To observe that my theory, so impudent in its address
To the Masters of Foetal Design and their perfect disciples,

Was rubbish — and leant to unfasten the window a notch —
When I suddenly grasped with aversion before I could see
it
The fact that the bed in the corner directly behind me
Had somebody in it. A little ginger chap,

Of the sort anthropologists group in the genus of *tramp*,
Was swaddled, as though with an eye to the state of the
sheets,
With half of his horrible self in the pouch of the bedspread
And half (both his raggled and poisonous trouser-legs) out;

Whose snore, like the rattle of bronchial stones in a
bucket,
Resounded the length and the depth and the breadth of
the problem
Of how to establish in safety a climate conducive
To kicking him out — till at last I could suffer no longer

The sight of his bundle of curls on my pillow, the proof
That even the worst of us look in our sleep like the angels
Except for a few. I closed to within a yard
And woke him, with a curt hurrahing sound.

And he reared in horror, like somebody late for work
Or a debutante subtly apprised of a welcome outstayed,
To demand (not of me, but more of the dreary familiar
Who exercised in its different styles the world's

Habit of persecution, and prodded him now)
Phit time is it? — so you'd think that it made any
difference —
So you'd think after all that the berth had a rota attached
And Ginger was wise to some cynical act of encroachment;

But when, with a plausible echo of fatherly firmness,
I answered, 'It's bedtime' — he popped out and stood in a
shiver,
And the released smell of his timid existence swirled
Like bracing coffee between our dissimilar stances.

Was there a dim recollection of tenement stairways
And jam and the Rangers possessed him, and sounded a
moment
In creaks of remorse? 'Ah'm sorry, son — Ah couldnae tell
They'd hae a wee boy sleepin here — ye know?'

(And I saw what a file of degradations queued
In his brown past, to explain how Jocky there
Could make me out to be innocent and wee:
As if to be wee was not to be dying of drink;

As if to be innocent meant that you still belonged
Where beds were made for one in particular.)
Still, the lifespan of sociable feelings is shortest of all
In the breast of the migrant Clydesider; and soon he
relapsed

Into patterns of favourite self-pitying sentiments. 'Son —
Ah'm warse than — Ah cannae, ye know? Ah'm off tae ma
dandy!
Ah've done a wee josie — aye wheesh! — it's warse what
Ah'm gettin —
Aye — warse!' And again the appeal to heredity — 'Son.'

(In the course of his speech, the imposter had gradually
settled
Back on the bed, and extended as visual aids
His knocked-about knuckles; tattooed with indelible
foresight
On one set of these was the purple imperative SAVE.)

Now I'm keen for all of us to be just as much worse as we
want,
In our own time and space — but not, after midnight, in
my bed;
And to keep his inertia at bay, I went for the parasite,
Scuttling him off with a shout and the push of a boot

That reminded his ribs I suppose of a Maryhill barman's,
Until I had driven him out of the door and his cough
Could be heard to deteriorate under a clock in the landing.
(Och, if he'd known *I* was Scottish! Then I'd have got it.)

*

But of course he came back in the night, when I dreamed
I was coughing
And he stood by the door in the composite guise of a
woman —
A mother, a doting landlady, a shadowy wife —
Sleepless as always, relieved nonetheless to have found
me,

Or half-relieved — given what I had become;
Saying — 'It's just from the coughing and so on I
wondered
If maybe a tramp had got into your bedroom' — and then,
Disappointedly: 'Couldn't you spare a wee thought for
your dad?'

(I thought I was dreaming again on the train in the
morning
To hear at my shoulder, before I had properly settled,
'Excuse me — is this seat taken?' spastically spoken;
But it wasn't our friend that I humoured through Didcot,
and Reading,

But an anoracked spotter of diesels from Sheffield
Whose mind was apparently out in the sidings at Crewe:
Only one more in a world of unwanted connexions,
Who waved like a child when I fled for the toilet at Ealing.)

*

This is my gloss on the story of Goldilocks. Note:
It uncovers a naked and difficult thought about beds,
Namely, that seldom again will there ever be one
With only you in it; take that however you will.

Jenny Joseph was a scholar at St Hilda's in Oxford and has worked as a newspaper reporter, a pub landlady and a lecturer. She won a Cholmondeley Award for her first collection, **The Unlooked-for Season**, published in 1960. **Persephone** (Bloodaxe, 1986) won the James Tait Black Memorial Prize. Her latest collection, **Ghosts and Other Company**, was published by Bloodaxe in 1995.

Uncartography

People on opposite shores
Crossing, recrossing;
The ferries always passing.

Like the story of the corn fox and hen
We are moved alternately towards each other
But never left near our food by the ferryman.

My map says
The years slide by as these banks do.
Unconfirmed against the real land
Is the map of love.

I wonder
Do the ferries still cross that far water
And what shores,
What shore unmappable of mind
Does your love lap now?

Piano practice exercises

Grey days grey days
Valley filled with mist
Brown trees empty trees
That once the sunlight kissed

Old dog finished dog
Slumped by the fire
Old man crippled man
Longing for desire

Now we climb the hill again
Through the evening rain
See again the lit-up town
Quivering on the plain

Some come up as we go on
Down the other side.
May they see the lights we know
Sparkling up the tide.

Dirge

You ask me not to write;
I quite see why.
You want no mourning:
I will not cry.

You want to hold the world
As you've always done
The way you think it should be,
Though it's gone.

Now you've relinquished
Even a ghostly eye
I write to you,
And I can cry.

Jackie Kay *was born in Scotland in 1961 and her first collection* **The Adoption Papers** *(Bloodaxe, 1991) won the Forward Poetry Prize, a Scottish Arts Council Book Award, the Saltire First Book of the Year Award and was shortlisted for the Mail on Sunday/John Llewellyn Rhys Prize. She has since published* **Other Lovers** *(Bloodaxe, 1993) and a collection of poems for children,* **Two's Company**, *now available in Puffin.*

Dance of the Cherry Blossom

Both of us are getting worse
Neither knows who had it first

He thinks I gave it to him
I think he gave it to me

Nights chasing clues where
One memory runs into another like dye.

Both of us are getting worse
I know I'm wasting precious time

But who did he meet between
May 87 and March 89.

I feel his breath on my back
A slow climb into himself then out.

In the morning it all seems different
Neither knows who had it first

We eat breakfast together — newspapers
And silence except for the slow slurp of tea

This companionship is better than anything
He thinks I gave it to him.

By lunchtime we're fighting over some petty thing
He tells me I've lost my sense of humour

I tell him I'm not Glaswegian
You all think death is a joke

It's not funny. I'm dying for fuck's sake
I think he gave it to me.

Just think he says it's every couple's dream
I won't have to wait for you up there

I'll have you night after night — your glorious legs
Your strong hard belly, your kissable cheeks

I cry when he says things like that
My shoulders cave in, my breathing trapped

Do you think you have a corner on dying
You self-pitying wretch, pathetic queen.

He pushes me; we roll on the floor like whirlwind;
When we are done in, our lips find each other

We touch soft as breeze, caress the small parts
Rocking back and forth, his arms become mine

There's nothing outside but the noise of the wind
The cherry blossom's dance through the night.

The Red Graveyard

There are some stones that open in the night like flowers
Down in the red graveyard where Bessie haunts her
lovers.
There are stones that shake and weep in the heart of night
Down in the red graveyard where Bessie haunts her
lovers.

Why do I remember the blues?
I am five or six or seven in the back garden;
the window is wide open;
her voice is slow motion through the heavy summer air.
Jelly roll. Kitchen man. Sausage roll. Frying pan.

Inside the house where I used to be myself,
her voice claims the rooms. In the best room even,
something has changed the shape of my silence.
Why do I remember her voice and not my own mother's?
Why do I remember the blues?

My mother's voice. What was it like?
A flat stone for skitting. An old rock.
Long long grass. Asphalt. Wind. Hail.
Cotton. Linen. Salt. Treacle.
I think it was a peach.
I heard it down to the ribbed stone.

I am coming down the stairs in my father's house.
I am five or six or seven. There is fat thick wallpaper
I always caress, bumping flower into flower
She is singing. (Did they play anyone else ever?)
My father's feet tap a shiny beat on the floor.

Christ, my father says, that's some voice she's got.
I pick up the record cover. And now. This is slow motion.
My hand swoops, glides, swoops again.
I pick up the cover and my fingers are all over her face.
Her black face. Her magnificent black face.
That's some voice. His shoes dancing on the floor.

There are some stones that open in the night like flowers
Down in the red graveyard where Bessie haunts her
lovers.
There are stones that shake and weep in the heart of night
Down in the red graveyard where Bessie haunts her
lovers.

Sassenachs

Me and my best pal (well, she was
till a minute ago) — are off to London.
First trip on an inter-city alone.
When we got on we were the same
kind of excited — jigging on our seats,
staring at everyone. But then,
I remembered I was to be sophisticated.
So when Jenny starts shouting,
'Look at that the land's flat already'
when we are just outside Glasgow
(Motherwell actually) I feel myself flush.
Or even worse, 'Sassenach country!
Wey Hey Hey.' The tartan tammy
sitting proudly on top of her pony;
the tartan scarf swinging like a tail.
The nose pressed to the window.
'England's not so beautiful, is it?'
And we haven't even crossed the border!

And the train's jazzy beat joins her:
Sassenachs sassenachs here we come.
Sassenachs sassenachs Rum Tum Tum
Sassenachs sassenachs how do you do.
SASSENACHS SASSENACHS WE'LL GET YOU!

Then she loses momentum, so out come
the egg mayonnaise sandwiches and
the big bottle of bru. 'My ma's done us proud,'
says Jenny, digging in, munching loud.
The whole train is an egg and I'm inside it.
I try and remain calm; Jenny starts it again,
Sassenachs sassenachs Rum Tum Tum.

Finally we get there: London, Euston;
and the very first person on the platform
gets asked — 'are you a genuine sassenach?'
I want to die, but instead I say, *'Jenny!'*
He replies in that English way —
'I beg your pardon,' and Jenny screams,
'Did you hear that Voice?'
And we both die laughing, clutching
our stomachs at Euston station.

Liz Lochhead is a dramatist, broadcaster and performing poet who was born in Motherwell and has spent most of her life in Glasgow. She was educated at the Glasgow School of Art and worked for eight years as an art teacher, before becoming a full-time writer in 1978.

What The Pool Said, On Midsummer's Day

I've led you by my garrulous banks, babbling
on and on till — drunk on air
and sure it's only water talking —
you come at last to my silence.
Listen, I'm dark
and still and deep enough.
Even this hottest gonging sun
on this longest day
can't white me out.
What are you waiting for?
I lie here, inviting, winking you in.

The woman was easy.
Like to like, I called her, she came.
In no time I had her
out of herself, slipping on my water-stockings,
leaning into, being cupped and clasped
in my green glass bra.
But it's you I want, and you know it, man.
I watch you, stripped, knee-deep
in my shallows, telling yourself
that what makes you gasp
and balls your gut
is not my coldness but your own fear.

71

— Your reasonable fear,
what's true in me admits it.
(Though deeper, oh
older than any reason).
Yes, I could
drown you, you
could foul my depths, it's not
unheard of. What's fish
in me could make flesh of you,
my wet weeds against your thigh, it
could turn nasty.
I could have you
gulping fistfuls fighting yourself
back from me.

I get darker and darker, suck harder.
On-the-brink man, you
wish I'd flash and dazzle again.
You'd make a fetish of zazzing dragonflies?
You want I should zip myself up
with the kingfisher's flightpath, be beautiful?
I say no tricks. I say just trust,
I'll soak through your skin and
slake your thirst.

I watch. You clench,
clench and come into me.

The Redneck

The day I got married I was like a rake.
Six months on the popcorn diet. Starving
but I wouldn't give the girls at work the satisfaction.
All so as I could swan down the aisle in my Scarlet O'Hara
towards that pig with a knife stuck down his sock.
Kilt suited him, but. Unlike ma da.
A toss-up between the Ancient Buchanan
and the Hunting MacIntyre.
I wanted tartan yes but no too roary.
State I was in everything had to be just so.
I had my mammy roasted in a pinwheel hat.
Ended up whole thing was nothing but a blur
and him shouting 'Perfect Working Order'
every two minutes mooning his mates
and flashing the photographer with his
Lion Rampant boxer shorts. A right rid neck.

During my marriage I ballooned.
None of a family thank God.
Bad enough splitting up without the complications.

Michael Longley was born in Belfast in 1939. His previous collections include **Poems 1963-83** and the acclaimed **Gorse Fires**, which won the 1991 Whitbread Poetry Award. He is married to the critic Edna Longley and they have three children. He recently retired from his post as Combined Arts Director at the Arts Council of Northern Ireland.

Snow Bunting
for Sarah

At Allaran, the otters' rock, between the breakers'
Uninterrupted rummaging and — from the duach —
Larksong, I mistake your voice for your mother's voice
Deciphering otter prints long before you were born

As though you were conceived in a hayfield so small
Stone walls surrounded a single stook, and the snow
Bunting's putative tinkle from beyond the ridge
Sounded even closer than the spindrift's whispering.

The Ice-Cream Man

Rum and raisin, vanilla, butter-scotch, walnut, peach:
You would rhyme off the flavours. That was before
They murdered the ice-cream man on the Lisburn Road
And you bought carnations to lay outside his shop.
I named for you all the wild flowers of the Burren
I had seen in one day: thyme, valerian, loosestrife,
Meadowsweet, tway blade, crowfoot, ling, angelica,
Herb robert, marjoram, cow parsley, sundew, vetch,
Mountain avens, wood sage, ragged robin, stitchwort,
Yarrow, lady's bedstraw, bindweed, bog pimpernel.

Badger
for Raymond Piper

I

Pushing the wedge of his body
Between cromlech and stone circle,
He excavates down mine shafts
And back into the depths of the hill.

His path straight and narrow
And not like the fox's zig-zags,
The arc of the hare who leaves
A silhouette on the sky line.

Night's silence around his shoulders,
His face lit by the moon, he
Manages the earth with his paws,
Returns underground to die.

II

An intestine taking in
patches of dog's-mercury,
brambles, the bluebell wood;
a heel revolving acorns;
a head with a price on it
brushing cuckoo-spit, goose-grass;
a name that parishes borrow.

III

For the digger, the earth-dog
It is a difficult delivery
Once the tongs take hold,

Vulnerable his pig's snout
That lifted cow-pats for beetles,
Hedgehogs for the soft meat,

His limbs dragging after them
So many stones turned over,
The trees they tilted.

*John Lucas is the author of **Studying Grosz on the Bus** (Peterloo Poets). He has also written several critical works, among them studies of Dickens and modern poetry. He was co-founder and editor of the Byron Press and until recently taught at Loughborough University. His versions of the poems of **Egil's Saga** have become classics. John Lucas lives in Beeston.*

Cheers

I'm drinking to this gnarled and stumpy bay tree
we brought home on our twenty-fifth anniversary.
A perfect one it looked then: thick-leaved, strong,
sure-rooted in its pot. Yet before long
the leaves began to wither, next to fall,
as though death had it marked, as though for all
our hopes, some worm or canker at its base
was working an unstoppable disease.

But still you fought to save it, kept from frost
the roots you'd fed, wouldn't believe it lost.
So, love, here's health! That after those hard years
our tree still lives, no longer shapely (shears
have seen to that), but stubbornly well-set,
and fit to last out many winters yet.

Arrivals

for Emma

In April on Campus Hill, looking down
where cagewheels span, an English professor guessed
"Eastwood? In that direction. Scruffy place,
or so I'm told," cigar jabbing due west.

So, here I was in the city of Gunn and Larwood,
Sherwood, Trent Bridge (the river no "cut-price Thames")
of Hilton, Byron, Kirk White, Sillitoe,
of Yates' and Boots: a city seamed with names.

From sober-sarky pub-talk I found out
that KIMBERLEY was "sweeter than a kiss,"
that HOME ALES summoned Arnold men from home,
and SHIPSTONES was anagram for "honest piss."

We studied maps, decoded agents' ads:
"Mature, well-sited" — — dry rot, ten miles out:
were told, "Bread-and-Lard Island, that's West Bridgford,
And them as live in the Park don't want for owt."

Long months of coppery sun, of grey-leaved streets,
we flew our high-pile dreams autumn brought down
with banker's flak: "a house is an investment!"
It meant mock-tudor in prim, dull Wollaton.

Soon, winter sealed off streets in ice and smog:
onion reek of hot-dog stalls, oil fumes
at Mount Street depot where young love shivered, chafed,
and filled last buses back to rented rooms.

Rantipole miners rode out to their night shifts,
trolley-bus upper decks steamy with song,
beer-breath, roll-ups and talk of Forest: "Grummitt
for England." "Owd yer tight." "'Night, youth." "S'long."

Then at Victoria Station pigeons swarmed
like premonitional smoke in its canopy
one evening as I leapt from the slowing train
back from a stint at Grantham's W.E.A.

— — and, yes, she was born that night. Out on the lawn
I raised a glass to the welcoming thick cope
of stars shook out across our midland sky,
and on the grass light glinted sharp as hope.

News From Nowhere

That rotting breath was cider
drunk to ease a cancered throat
though pain sharpened his eyes
to vistas lost from trudged streets

where still he fattened dreams for Xmas cheer:
"String the bloody tories from lamp-posts
with gold balls rammed in their mouths."
A year later that voice

like kerb-roughened steel came growling
"another poxy day in this blighted place,"
then, turning against my shrug — —
"the right weather for no-hopers."

One morning he was missing. "Next
Door was forced to break in. Well,
he'd nothing much to live for,"
was all our new, young postman said.

That night I dreamed of messages
brought from some beleaguered state
whose wind-torn shutters rasped
of broken cities to be re-built,

and through next morning's drizzle
of news was listening still
for his incurable sound,
his wakening words.

Roger McGough *was born in Liverpool and, with Adrian Henri and Brian Patten, was the author of the hugely influential* **Mersey Sound** *(Penguin, 1967). He has published many collections of poetry for children and adults and is an accomplished performer of his own work. Two volumes of his selected poems from 1967-87,* **Blazing Fruit** *and* **You At The Back** *are published by Penguin and his work appears in* **Penguin Modern Poets 4** *(1995).*

Defying Gravity

Gravity is one of the oldest tricks in the book.
Let go of the book and it abseils to the ground
As if, at the centre of the earth, spins a giant yo-yo
To which everything is attached by an invisible string.

Tear out a page of the book and make an aeroplane.
Launch it. For an instant it seems that you have fashioned
A shape that can outwit air, that has slipped the knot.
But no. The earth turns, the winch tightens, it is wound
in.

One of my closest friends is, at the time of writing,
Attempting to defy gravity, and will surely succeed.
Eighteen months ago he was playing rugby,
Now, seven stones lighter, his wife carries him aw-

Kwardly from room to room. Arranges him gently
Upon the sofa for the visitors. 'How are things?'
Asks one, not wanting to know. Pause. 'Not too bad.'
(Open brackets. Condition inoperable. Close brackets.)

Soon now, the man that I love (not the armful of bones)
Will defy gravity. Freeing himself from the tackle
He will sidestep the opposition and streak down the wing
Towards a dimension as yet unimagined.

Back where the strings are attached there will be a service
And homage paid to the giant yo-yo. A box of left-overs
Will be lowered into a space on loan from the clay.
Then, weighted down, the living will walk wearily away.

Ian McMillan *was born in 1956 and has been a full-time writer and performer since 1981. He works extensively in radio and has recently been described in The Times as "intelligent if not always intelligible!"*

Kake Yourself Comfortable

Kome in. Sit Kown.
Kake yourself comfortable.

Kup of Kea? Bit of Kake?
Kilk? Kugar?

My problem? You Kish
to Kiscuss it?

Ah yes. The letter K.
Well, Kit all goes back

Ko Ky Khildhood. We were
very Koor. I only had one

Koy. A building Krick with
Ketters on. Except all the

Ketters had Keen Kubbed off,
except one. All my childhood

I Konly Kever saw Kone letter.
The letter S.

Dad, the Donkey's on Fire

There is a burning donkey
at the side of the canal.
It lights up the sky.

Look at the burning donkey.
In Donkey Language it is saying
'Look at me, you bastards,

I am on fire.'
Although it sounds like hee haw.

Death's Feet

I don't know. Sometimes you lie
and then you call it art. The man said
'Are you working on a novel?' and

I said, YES, O YES, YES I AM, YES.
And he said 'I hope it's one of your
Inspector McMillan novels. I just

love his jutting jaw, and the way
he solves it on the penultimate
page,leaving the last page free

for recipes.' And I said YES O YES
AYE AR THIS IS IT PAL AYE AR YES.
And he said 'Do you have a title

for it?' And I coughed and said
COUGH ER AR TITLE AR WELL THA
KNOWS SEMMAS COUGH ER death's feet.

come stalky stalky
up the path
feeling your tie
in the moon's pale light.

Wes Magee was born in 1939 in Greenock, Scotland. He is a former teacher and headteacher who has been a full-time author since 1989. Wes Magee has published four collections for adults and more than forty books for young readers, including poetry, fiction and plays.

In The Castle Of Gloom

 Oh,
 it's cold,
it's as cold as a tomb,
 and
 it's dark
as a windowless room
 in
 the Castle,
the Castle of Gloom.

  (meet your dooooom)

No sun through the shutters.
No candle flame gutters.
No log embers glimmer.
No silver plates shimmer.
 No lamps in the hall.
 No brands on the wall.
 No moonbeams at night.
 No starshine.
  No light.

Oh,
  it's cold,
it's as cold as a tomb,
  and
  it's dark
as a windowless room
  in
  the Castle,
the Castle of Gloom.

(<u>meet your doooooooooom</u>)

Our Miss Gill and Mr Scott

Our Miss Gill
and Mr Scott
seem to like each other
rather a lot.
His class
and our class
are always going
on trips together.
Today we climbed
Tucker's Hill
in <u>dreadful</u> weather.
  "He held her hand."
  "Never!"
  "He did, and they kissed."
  "No!"
It turned terribly cold.
"I'm freezing," said Jill.
It started to rain,
then there was sleet
and then there was snow.

At least it was warm
on the coach
and we all sang.
Arrived at the school gate
just as the bell rang.
Off we trooped home.
At the street corner
I turned
and looked back.
So did Jill.
We watched
as our Miss Gill
crossed the car park
hand in glove
with Mr Scott.
   "They <u>are</u> in love,"
said Jill.
Yes, they do seem
to like each other
rather a lot.

Adrian Mitchell *was born in London in 1932. He was one of the leaders of the revival in oral poetry in the late 1950s and 60s and has since become one of Europe's best-selling poets. He has written plays for the stage, radio and television, and is the author of a number of novels for adults and children. He is a Fellow of the Royal Society of Literature.*

Beattie Is Three

At the top of the stairs
I ask for her hand. O.K.
She gives it to me.
How her fist fits my palm,
A bunch of consolation.
We take our time
Down the steep carpetway
As I wish silently
That the stairs were endless.

Back in the Playground Blues

I dreamed I was back in the playground, I was about four
feet high
Yes dreamed I was back in the playground, standing about
four feet high
Well the playground was three miles long and the
playground was five miles wide

It was broken black tarmac with a high wire fence all
around
Broken black dusty tarmac with a high fence running all
around
And it had a special name to it, they called it The Killing
Ground

Got a mother and a father, they're one thousand years
away
The rulers of The Killing Ground are coming out to play
Everybody thinking: 'Who they going to play with today?'

  Well you get it for being Jewish
  And you get it for being black
  Get it for being chicken
  And you get it for fighting back
  You get it for being big and fat
  Get it for being small
  Oh those who get it get it and get it
  For any damn thing at all

Sometimes they take a beetle, tear off its six legs one by
one
Beetle on its black back, rocking in the lunchtime sun
But a beetle can't beg for mercy, a beetle's not half the fun

I heard a deep voice talking, it had that iceberg sound
'It prepares them for Life' — but I have never found
Any place in my life worse than The Killing Ground.

Stufferation

Lovers lie around in it
Broken glass is found in it
Grass
I like that stuff

Tuna fish get trapped in it
Legs come wrapped in it
Nylon
I like that stuff

Eskimos and tramps chew it
Madam Tussaud gave status to it
Wax
I like that stuff

Elephants get sprayed with it
Scotch is made with it
Water
I like that stuff

Clergy are dumbfounded by it
Bones are surrounded by it
Flesh
I like that stuff

Harps are strung with it
Mattresses are sprung with it
Wire
I like that stuff

Carpenters make cots of it
Undertakers use lots of it
Wood
I like that stuff

Cigarettes are lit by it
Pensioners get happy when they sit by it
Fire
I like that stuff

Dankworth's alto is made of it, most of it,
Scoobdidoo is composed of it
Plastic
I like that stuff

Apemen take it to make them hairier
I ate a ton of it in Bulgaria
Yoghurt
I like that stuff

Man-made fibres and raw materials
Old rolled gold and breakfast cereals
Platinum linoleum
I like that stuff

Skin on my hands
Hair on my head
Toenails on my feet
And linen on the bed

Well I like that stuff
Yes I like that stuff
The earth
Is made of earth
And I like that stuff

Henry Normal was born in Carlton, Nottingham. He has gained a huge following as a performance poet and as a stand-up alternative comedian. He was the originator, star and co-writer of Channel Four's **Packet of Three** and presented his live poetry series **Encyclopaedia Poetica** on BBC Radio 4. Henry Normal has collaborated in writing and performing with Steve Coogan and his screenwriting has brought him a BAFTA award.

The Eating of a Unicorn

So I'm eating this unicorn and I'm thinking this isn't right
But you've got to eat haven't you?
So you tell yourself it's OK everybody eats them
But you know that's not strictly true
So you look for some justification, some strand of logic,
Some attitude, some philosophy, however slim
But you know in your gut it still isn't right
So you think about minimising the damage
But you know you can't simply throw up and piece the whole
Business back together
So you say what is done is done and you have to live with it
But you still wish you hadn't eaten the bloody thing
And wonder how you could have ever felt that hungry
Or thought it a good idea
So you try to pretend it never happened,
That you know nothing about it
And that besides you thought it was just a horse made up
But now you have to dispose of the body and in case it's
Discovered you have to hide the head and the horn separate

So there you are breaking off the head and the horn
From a half-eaten unicorn at dead of night
But...

The Frame of the Mona Lisa Dreams

Though you have looked in my direction many times
You do not remember me
Set on a wall on my own
You would not exalt me

I have intrinsic value

But this notoriety is not of my own making
I have seen eyes filled with wonder glance over me

Like the plain sister
I see all
But am not seen
The curious and the cynical I see
The desperate and the disappointed I see

Like the assassin my fame is a reflection
Like the bodyguard I am expendable
I know my place at court

And in all the borrowed light shined upon me
From my vantage at the edge of the glare
Occasionally I see refracted
In the tiring of a gaze
Something of myself

A gentle sob
Almost, yet not quite, lost

Remember me

It seems to say

Remember me

And I will remember you.

Brian Patten was born in Liverpool in 1946 and was responsible, with Adrian Henri and Roger McGough, for reviving the popularity of poetry in performance. Brian Patten's work has been translated into many languages and he is the author of several critically-acclaimed collections of poetry for adults and children.

A Blade of Grass

You ask for a poem.
I offer you a blade of grass.
You say it is not good enough.
You ask for a poem.

I say this blade of grass will do.
It has dressed itself in frost,
It is more immediate
Than any image of my making.

You say it is not a poem.
It is a blade of grass and grass
Is not quite good enough.
I offer you a blade of grass.

You are indignant.
You say it is too easy to offer grass.
It is absurd.
Anyone can offer a blade of grass.

You ask for a poem.
And so I write you a tragedy about
How a blade of grass
Becomes more and more difficult to offer,

And about how as you grow older
A blade of grass
Becomes more difficult to accept.

The Ambush

When the face you swore never to forget
Can no longer be remembered,
When a list of regrets are torn up and thrown away
Then the hurt fades,
And you think you've grown strong.
You sit in bars and boast to yourself,
'Never again will I be vulnerable.
It was an aberration to be so open,
A folly, never to be repeated.'
How absurd and fragile such promises.
Hidden from you, crouched
Among the longings you have suppressed
And the desires you imagine tamed,
A sweet pain waits in ambush.
And there will come a day when in a field
Heaven's mouth gapes open,
And on a web the shadow
Of a marigold will smoulder.
Then without warning,
Without a shred of comfort,
Emotions you thought had been put aside
Will flare up within you and bleed you of reason.
The routines which comforted you,
And the habits in which you sought refuge
Will bend like sunlight under water,
And go astray.
Your body will become a banquet,

Falling heavenwards,
You will loll in spring's sweet avalanche
Without the burden of memory,
And once again
Monstrous love will swallow you.

The Last Gift

For Heinz Henghes

H.H.   *'What's the story about?'*
B.P.   *'About a mouse that gets eaten by an eagle.'*
H.H.   *'Poor mouse.'*
B.P.   *'No, the mouse becomes part of the eagle.'*
H.H.   *'Lucky mouse. Perhaps I'll be that lucky.'*

Perhaps next time he will be
A musician playing in a hall in which
A few children will fidget and dream
While the crowd regrets
What cannot help but pass.
Or perhaps he will be something a snowdrift's buried
And that's not found again,
Or the contradiction of blossom
On a stunted apple-tree.

Perhaps, but all I know for certain
Is that already some friends are in their graves,
And for them the world is no longer fixed
In its stubborn details.
Astonished in moments of clarity to realise
How all that surrounds me has passed
Again and again through death,
I still strut without understanding
Between an entrance of skin and an exit of soil.

It is too much to expect he will come back
In the same form,
Molecule by sweet molecule reassembled.

When the grave pushes him back up
Into the blood or the tongue of a sparrow,
When he becomes the scent of foxglove,
Becomes fish or glow-worm,
When as a mole he nuzzles his way up
Eating worms that once budded inside him,
It's too much to expect that I'll still be around.

I'll not be here when he comes back
As a moth with no memory of flames.

It is a dubious honour getting to know the dead,
Knowing them on more intimate terms,
Friends who come and go in what at the last moment
Seems hardly a moment.
And now as one by dreamless one they are dropped
Into the never distant, dreamless grave,
As individual memory fades
And eye-bewildering light is put aside,
We grow more baffled by this last
Gift of the days they are denied.

Tom Paulin *was born in Leeds in 1949 and grew up in Belfast, educated at the Universities of Hull and Oxford and taught for some years at Nottingham University. Tom Paulin is a Fellow of Hertford College, Oxford and is G.M. Young Lecturer in English Literature at Oxford University.*

Matins

A tinniness in that bell
— I was ten when I heard it first
its sad but urgent tang
binging across two dead —
you could hardly call them fields
and there it goes again
off-key but beating out
its meek unsettled belief
on a shore of this small republic
not a *cloche felee* for sure
just Anglican Irish and poor

maybe I'll cross those acres
— deadness and brambles just
between our house and the church?
go into that half-strange porch
its odour of damp and limewash
strawbottomed chairs and slack
well loose little case of hymnals
it must be a tribal thing
this wanting to go back there
(d'you want to kneel in prayer?)
this wishing the words were firm
with a bit of a kick and a skip
why couldn't they stay the same
and sing *bing-ding bing-ding*?

Klee/Clover

Nightwatch after nightwatch
Paul Klee endured
'horribly boring guard duty'
at the gasoline cellar
and every morning
outside the Zeppelin hangar
there was drill then a speech
tacked with junk formulas
he varnished wings
and stencilled numbers
next to gothic insignia
a private first-class
with a lippy dislike
of their royal majesties
and *Flying School 5 (Bavaria)*

he wrote home to Lily
it's nice this spring weather
and now we've laid out a garden
between the second and third runways
the airfield's becoming
more and more beautiful

Each time a plane crashed
— and that happened quite often
he cut squares of canvas
from the wings and fuselage
he never said why
but every smashed biplane
looked daft or ridiculous
halfjoky and untrue
— maybe the pilots annoyed him?
those unlovely aristos
who never knew they were flying
primed blank canvases
into his beautiful airfield

A New Society

It's easy enough to regret them when they're gone.
Beds creaked on boards in the brick meadows
Somewhere above a tired earth no one had seen
Since Arkwright became a street name.

Their boxed rooms were papered with generations,
There were gas lamps, corner shops that smelt of wrapped bread,
Worn thresholds warmed by the sun and kids playing ball
Near the odd, black, Ford Popular.

Then they were empty like plague streets, their doors barred
And windows zinced. Dead lids weighted with coins,
Dead ends all of them when their families left.
Then broken terraces carried away in skips.

A man squints down a theodolite, others stretch white tapes
Over the humped soil or dig trenches that are like useful graves.
Diesel combusts as yellow bulldozers push earth
With their shields. Piledrivers thud on opened ground.

Just watching this — the laid-out streets, the mixers
Churning cement, the new bricks rising on their foundations —
Makes me want to believe in some undoctrinaire
Statement of what should be. A factual idealism.

A mummified Bentham should flourish in this soil
And unfold an order that's unaggressively civilian,
Where taps gush water into stainless sinks
And there's a smell of fresh paint in sunlit kitchens.

Where rats are destroyed and crawlies discouraged,
Where the Law is glimpsed on occasional traffic duties
And the streets are friendly with surprise recognitions.
Where, besides these, there's a visible water

That lets the sun dazzle on Bank Holidays, and where kids
Can paddle safely. There should be some grass, too,
And the chance of an unremarkable privacy,
A vegetable silence there for the taking.

Nigel Planer is a versatile actor and writer who first achieved fame for his role as Neil in The Young Ones. He has quickly gained a considerable reputation as a poet and a performer of his own work.

Assuming you go first

When you've become a will and a jar of bits,
am I going to incinerate myself, the way it hits
some people? Or were they wasted, the years to please you,
opportunities and proper lives I missed?
But when I'm pissed it all comes out, I cry,
"please don't die."

I always think of the time with you as night,
and chocolate conversation, and clever candle-light,
that flatters. And all that mess, and the stress
of your dogs and broken buildings and teenage junk,
and I'm a skunk to get this drunk, and I cry,
"please don't die."

On the plane back from some island where it's hot,
I wondered whether I'd be frightened or not
if we crashed. And thought it would be OK, today,
to plummet together, your dress was exotic floral,
But when the alcohol level is high, I cry.
Please don't die.

Rage, rage (against the designing of the life)

Personally speaking, I don't give a fuck about our curtain
material,
And I could make do with any kind of sofa, or lampshade,
Or pillow covering, so I don't know why I bother
To spend my Saturdays farting around with a credit card,
Pretending I'm not counting up how much we've paid
For the latest Conran wicker basket, or another
Bloody wrought iron candlestick, I only know I must be on
my guard
Against overspending.

Oh sure, I like being thought successful,
And I do like having a presentable home
And people saying "how fantastic" when they come to see
us,
And asking where we got our chairs.
And there is a nasty satisfaction as they roam
Around the flat, knowing some of them would like to be us,
But it costs a lot, this putting on of airs,
And I can't help tending

To think, for fuck's sake what does it matter?
At the heart of it there's the usual grief,
For which expensive fabrics and colour co-ordination
cannot compensate,
And which, I think, the paying of the bills makes easier to
see,
And which maybe even advertises our need for some relief
From the endless, mind-numbing and excruciating
boredom of familial responsibility.
You can have just as bad a time

In beautiful surroundings as in a crusty dump.
Not being a behaviourist, I don't believe that crockery

From Villeroy-Bosch will make a meal taste right,
Or serve any purpose other than to be dishwasher
friendly.
Sometimes I feel that these designers make a mockery
Of us, and I wander, flicking ash, around the flat at night.
When up against such costly candy-floss, one has to be
intentionally
Childish, and commit a crime.

Peter Porter *is an Australian-born poet, long resident in Britain. He was born in 1929. After a variety of jobs, including bookselling and advertising writing, he has been a freelance literary journalist in London since 1968. Peter Porter has published 14 volumes of verse, most recently* **Collected Poems** *(1983),* **The Chair of Babel** *(1992) and* **Millenial Fables** *(1994). He has two grown-up daughters.*

Doll's House

Against the haunting of our cats,
Shy raids by children visiting, it stays
 As truthful as the willow flats
  Which blocked her days.

Its owner slammed the door and fled
Like Nora to the liberal hinterland.
 What could resite that jostled bed?
  No grown-up hand.

The miniature hoover lies
Brim-full of dust, the chest-of-drawers gapes;
 On holidays a sobbing tries
  To fluff the drapes.

And now to play at house you need
Another sort of house inside your head
 Where duty states you soothe and feed
  The plastic dead.

Her children have outgrown it too,
But do they hear the twisting of the key,
  Entail their ruined space in lieu
    Of charity?

Love, orderer of dolls and towns,
Has Liliputianized the scale of pain,
  So the wide adult eye looks down,
    Bereaved again

Of esperance, the childhood flush,
And has no passage into afternoons
  But through diminished doors and hush
    Of darkened rooms.

Throw the Book at Them

Where do we go to live? We're born ticking
on the page and from the first disclosure on
we sense that time is useless without fear.
So here must gather all those claques of fact
we make good use of — and what are they
but words? Imagine the tight nucleus we know
is true inheritance: we find nothing more
to do with it than turn it back to chaos.
Proust could get ten thousand lines from
one night at a party and Robert Browning
knew he was in love only when he found he'd
said so on the page. How Elizabeth
loved his profile when it hovered over her
in trochees. Personification's special dangers
outweighed Daddy's growlings and the bladder
weakness of poor Flush. Rochefoucauld
spoiled things with his fully-frontal maxim:

it's all much cooler really, exile under cypresses
and chatting at the well, but never far
from the cherished self-immersing diaries —
no matter how fast they fill, white paper presses
on the eyes of nightmare and the black dog
barks defensively. There are mornings
in the bathroom when a wonky razor seems
pons asinorum of responsibility,
but don't despair, a brush with life's not final
till it's found a way to do the rope trick
with dependent clauses. Dying's a book
with uncut pages; the pentel scurries and the tea
grows cold, and back in London a publisher
announces a burnished tome on Tuscany.
To get through life, just join the dots up, they
may prove a subcutaneous punctuation.
Today in Rouen there is an Avenue
Gustave Flaubert, but nothing spoils the stillness
at his desk. The DPP has all he needs
to start the trial — the boys in blue, the talkative
punk witnesses slurping from chipped cups.
The rules remain: you are the books you write.

In Rosewell

These small, well-built and greystone Lothian houses
Seem full of sadness, ringed about by sky.
Unlike the flock of birds my presence rouses
Their dignity will wait till I go by.
Perhaps they feel that one who lives in books
Is hardly worth a turbulence of rooks.

The birds have high trees and a castled river
To underwrite their screaming senate's noise
As down the wet roads juggernauts deliver
Animals to death, and cycling boys
Pass kennels where impounded dogs and cats
Howl to the lonely lawns and council flats.

How should a writer better test self-pity
Than standing soaked outside the Miners' Club
With letters of importance for some city
And far too shy to go into the pub?
I bring my quiet burden to the post,
A lifetime's correspondence with a ghost.

And No Help Came

Where would you look for blessing who are caught
In published acres of millennia
By ravishment of salt and raucous saints
Or janissaries drilling a Big Bang?
The parish of the poor you'd seek, far from
The high grandstands of words and notes and paints.

And when you drove your flagged and honking jeep
Among the huts of starving, brutalized
Dependents, you might chance to hear them playing
Sentimental songs of flowers and moons
Chiefly to keep them safe from art, whose gods
Build palaces adorned with scenes of flaying.

Peter Redgrove read science at Cambridge and has worked as a research scientist and scientific journalist. He trained as a lay analyst with Dr. John Layard. He has published twenty-three books of verse and seven novels. Currently he is engaged on a study of Mesmerism, sexuality and poetry with the working title — **Lucid Orgasm**.

At the Edge of the Wood

First, boys out of school went out of their way home
To detonate the windows; at each smash
Piping with delight and skipping for fright
Of a ghost of the old man popping over his hedge,
Shrieking and nodding from the gate.
Then the game palled, since it was only breaking the silence.
The rain sluiced through the starred gaps,
Crept up walls and into the brick; frost bit and munched;
Weeds craned in and leant on the doors.
Now it is a plot without trees let into the wood
Piled high with tangle and tousle
Buried parapets and roots picking at the last mortar
Though the chimney still stands sheathed in leaves
And you can see for the time being where in a nook
A briony bursts its pot with a shower of roots
And back through the press of shrubs and stems
Deep-coils into the woods.

Orchard With Wasps

The rouged fruits in
The orchard by the waterfall, the bronzed fruits,

The brassy flush on the apples.
He gripped the fruit

And it buzzed like a gong stilled with his fingers
And a wasp flew out with its note

From the gong of sugar and scented rain
All the gongs shining like big rain under the trees

Within the sound of the little waterfall
Like a gash in the apple-flesh of time

Streaming with its juices and bruised.
Such a wasp, so full of sugar

Flew out within the sound
Of the apple-scented waterfall,

Such a gondola of yellow rooms
Striped with black rooms

Fuelled with syrups hovering
At the point of crystal,

Applegenius, loverwasp, scimitar
Of scented air and sugar-energy

Shining up his lamp-tree tall and devious
Given utterly to its transformations

From sharp-scented flowers to honey-gongs,
Giver and taker of pollination-favours,

A small price for such syrups and plunderings,
Its barky flesh, its beckoning fruit,

Its deep odour of cider and withering grasses,
Its brassy bottles and its Aladdin gold-black drunks.

Christopher Reid *is Poetry Editor at Faber and Faber. His work has been acknowledged with the award of the Hawthornden Prize, a Gregory Award and the Somerset Maugham Award.*

An Angel

An angel flew by
and the electricity dimmed.
It was like a soft jolt
to the whole of being.
I raised my eyes from the poems
that lay on the kitchen table,
the work of a friend, now dead.

It should not have mattered.
As the light glowed again,
I ought to have continued reading,
but that single pause
terrified me.
We say of the old
that they tremble on the brink.
I found that I was trembling.

Perhaps the black country nights
Encourage superstition.
I remembered the angels
that had visited people I knew,
not hurrying past them
and merely stirring the air,
but descending with the all-inclusive
wingspan of annunciation
to obliterate them totally —
and I rose to my feet.

That one brief indecision
of the electric light
in a night of solitude
showed me how weak I was.
The poems on the table
lay where I had left them,
not knowing they had been abandoned.

A Box

Imagine a box, not a very big one,
but containing the following indispensable items:
a bed, a soup bowl, a landscape of mists and birches,
the words spoken by a pensive mother,
the absence of a father, several books including
a dictionary with a torn spine
and the works of the troubadours, a small photograph
in which the wince of a girl in sunlight is the main

                                                 point,

a document with a stamp and a signature,
a message received from the friend of a friend,
a journey by train, an odd-looking parcel,
some jokes, anxiety and a final revelation.
Imagine this box, which should not be too large,
then take it and hide it with as little fuss as you can
somewhere you know its contents will be safe.

Vernon Scannell, born in 1922, lived in Beeston as a small boy and remembers it with affection. His poems have won various prizes, the Heinemann Award for Literature, The Cholmondeley Poetry Prize and The Society of Authors Travelling Scholarship. He is a Fellow of the Royal Society of Literature.

A Case of Murder

They should not have left him there alone,
Alone that is except for the cat.
He was only nine, not old enough
To be left alone in a basement flat,
Alone, that is, except for the cat.
A dog would have been a different thing,
A big gruff dog with slashing jaws,
But a cat with round eyes mad as gold,
Plump as a cushion with tucked-in paws —
Better have left him with a fair-sized rat!
But what they did was leave him with a cat.
He hated that cat; he watched it sit,
A buzzing machine of soft black stuff,
He sat and watched and he hated it,
Snug in its fur, hot blood in a muff,
And its mad gold stare and the way it sat
Crooning dark warmth: he loathed all that.
So he took Daddy's stick and he hit the cat.
Then quick as a sudden crack in glass
It hissed, black flash, to a hiding place
In the dust and dark beneath the couch,
And he followed the grin on his new-made face,
A wide-eyed, frightened snarl of a grin,
And he took the stick and he thrust it in,

116

Hard and quick in the furry dark.
The black fur squealed and he felt his skin
Prickle with sparks of dry delight.
Then the cat again came into sight,
Shot for the door that wasn't quite shut,
But the boy, quick too, slammed fast the door:
The cat, half-through, was cracked like a nut
And the soft black thud was dumped on the floor.
Then the boy was suddenly terrified
And he bit his knuckles and cried and cried;
But he had to do something with the dead thing there.
His eyes squeezed beads of salty prayer
But the wound of fear gaped wide and raw;
He dared not touch the thing with his hands
So he fetched a spade and shovelled it
And dumped the load of heavy fur
In the spidery cupboard under the stair
Where it's been for years, and though it died
It's grown in that cupboard and its hot low purr
Grows slowly louder year by year:
There'll not be a corner for the boy to hide
When the cupboard swells and all sides split
And the huge black cat pads out of it.

Two Variations on an Old Theme

I

Winter returns, white with patient rage;
Its peckish minutes nibble at my skin.
I am not old enough to cope with age.

Most men mature, grow stoical and sage,
Don't flinch when, as the knives of ice go in,
Winter returns, white with patient rage.

But somehow I have never reached the stage
Where I can take time's punches on the chin;
I am not old enough to cope with age.

No games divert, no medicines assuage
The pain and fear; my overcoat is thin.
Winter returns, white with patient rage.

Mordacious winds come howling from their cage.
There's no escape, I'm pinioned by their din.
I am not old enough to cope with age.

The little space left on the final page
Attends words like 'deceased' and 'next of kin'.
Winter returns, white with patient rage;
I am not old enough to cope with age.

II

It has to come, I know, but I need time;
I'm not prepared; I've got so much to learn.
I couldn't face it with a face like mine.

The soldier is conditioned by his trade:
He treats the whole thing as a family joke.
The airman tells me it's a piece of cake.

The gaunt religious welcomes it with joy,
Flings wizened arms ecstatically wide
And swallow-dives into the awful void.

Gangsters, cops and nurses every day
Observe its policies without a qualm;
For them the end's the last move in a game.

But wait a minute! What about the kids,
Twelve-year-olds, scared aunties, timorous clerks?
All have faced it; surely they've no tricks
I'm unaware of that could make it seem
Less terrible? No, no, yet most have made
Astonishingly little fuss indeed.

If they can take it, there's no reason why
I shouldn't too. I'll be okay, I know —
Oh Christ, I'll always be too young to die!

Penelope Shuttle's sixth collection of poetry, **Building a City for Jamie**, was published by OUP in May 1996. She is co-author with Peter Redgrove of **The Wise Wound**, their ground-breaking study of menstrual psychology (in print since 1978) and its 1995 sequel, **Alchemy for Women**. Her stories have appeared in The London Magazine, Metropolitan and Passport. She is presently working on a novel.

Big Cat

A windowful of cloud.
Rain on the big sloping glass roof
falls from a once-only sky.

The lovers shiver,
their tongues spate
in their mouths
with a why and a how;
they say now, now.

The room hold them in its history,
between its pages,
as they tap at heaven.

They shake in their silver lining.

The window holds its breath.

Then the lovers come.
Then sleep purrs in their throats
like a big cat guessing names.

Georgette

No matter how often she moves the furniture
she can't find her Childhood.
It is named after the fashion of hurricanes,
Childhood Georgette.
But where is it?
No matter how often she coaxes old chairs
into new places, she can't find her Childhood.
Father grumbles quietly up and down the steps.
Mussed and sweaty,
she pushes everything back against the walls.
She looks and looks. Childhood?
Big hands clap the sky, Father is sending the rain.
She pushes her little foster bike through the rooms,
searching.
Father is at the window with his stormy thoughts.
He is shaking his branches.
Too old for a kiss? laughs Father out in the rain.
Again and again
he and the rain know what's right and what's wrong.
She leans the tear-stained bike against the wall.
Childhood?
A nudge of thunder. Don't tell lies!
She puts the furniture back how it was, everything
stares back obediently at her. Father
is muttering one of his old songs
and peeping round the door. Rain calls
out the name she never liked.
The windows don't lift a finger. Now Father
in those mirrors
is smiling at his little poupee.
Now she rides on Father's shoulders,
seeing everything, interpreting nothing.
Georgette is riding. Ice and rain on the stairs,
all the rooms galloping round and round
and hurting, Father knows where her Childhood is.

My Moon

My moon goes everywhere.
My moon is happy because you are sleeping
and dreaming.
My moon is beyond pines and firs.
My moon is blue shadow under almond trees.
My moon has a flair for silence.
My moon plans the wedding day of honey and rain.
My moon loves to pilgrimage,
skimming hill and field
and coming home to me.

Dreaming of my moon,
I slide down her bosom of outstanding scenery,
her belly of whiteness.

My moon is sweet water I wash in.
I am always her last word.

Jon Silkin's most recent collections of verse are: **The Lens-Breakers** (Sinclair-Stevenson, 1992) and **Selected Poems** (also Sinclair-Stevenson 1994). He has edited **The Penguin Book of First World War Poetry**, and, with Jon Glover, **The Penguin Book of First World War Prose**. He has published with Sinclair-Stevenson **Wilfred Owen:the War Poems** (1994). His collection **Nature With Man** was awarded the Geoffrey Faber Memorial Prize in 1966. He co-edits the literary quarterly **Stand**. He is a Fellow of the Royal Society of Literature. He has recently published a long poem with drafts called **Watersmeet** (Bay Press, 1995).

Death of a Son
(Who died in a mental hospital aged one)

Something has ceased to come along with me.
Something like a person: something very like one.
   And there was no nobility in it
     Or anything like that.

Something was there like a one year
Old house, dumb as stone. While the near buildings
   Sang like birds and laughed
     Understanding the pact

They were to have with silence. But he
Neither sang nor laughed. He did not bless silence
   Like bread, with words.
     He did not forsake silence.

But rather, like a house in mourning
Kept the eye turned in to watch the silence while
  The other houses like birds
  Sang around him.

And the breathing silence neither
Moved nor was still.

 I have seen stones: I have seen brick
But this house was made up of neither bricks nor stone
  But a house of flesh and blood
  With flesh of stone

 And bricks for blood. A house
Of stones and blood in breathing silence with the other
  Birds singing crazy on its chimneys.
  But this was silence,

 This was something else, this was
Hearing and speaking though he was a house drawn
  Into silence, this was
  Something religious in his silence,

 Something shining in his quiet,
This was different, this was altogether something else:
  Though he never spoke, this
  Was something to do with death.

 And then slowly the eye stopped looking
Inward. The silence rose and became still.
The look turned to the outer place and stopped,
  With the birds still shrilling around him.
  And as if he could speak

He turned over on his side with his one year
Red as a wound
He turned over as if he could be sorry for this
And out of his eyes two great tears rolled, like stones, and
  he died.

Harebell

The harebell is one flower,
Its solitariness
Bespoke by its colour, not blue
Nor violet; hovering between, precisely.
It is a spare delicate bell.
Inside it are three pale sugary stigmas welded
To each other at equal angles,
Not seen until looked for.
Its stem is thin as wire.
The flower looks down, and if
Lifted, looks fixedly
At the admirer.
Its silence halted between primness and beauty,
Its shape is wrung from the sounds of life round it
As a bell's sound forms the bell's shape from silence,
and resumes its demure integrity;
More precise, more shaped, than the bluebell;
More venturesome. More stirred, ungarrulous.
Stern as a pin.

*Ken Smith is the author of sundry collections of poetry from Bloodaxe, the latest of which is **Tender to the Queen of Spain**, and two non-fiction works — **Inside Time** and **Berlin Coming in from the Cold**.*

Sunk Island, that winter

'O westron wind when wilt thou blow
And the small rain down shall rain'

O that my love O that
my love: the wind,
the reeds, the telephone wire
and I, all singing.

It's late afternoon
in a flat country,
the sea birds rise
far off and fall quietly.

But the sea goes away
leaving these fields,
this tall yellow marsh grass
and the small trees blown inland.

And last winter the gale
lifted the pigsty roof, the geese
blew out to sea, the bell
on the dull swell of the Humber

clanked through my dream
of hills in my own land.
Perhaps I am leaving,
a man stung by his woman's scolding.

Perhaps nothing. Or drunk
going home by the ditches,
singing, from a neighbour's house,
a man at the end of himself

where there's only the sea
on the sea, each thing at a distance:
dutch barn, brick letter-box,
wall of the house I will sleep in.

Yuppy Love

What he calls her: my little pocket calculator
my fully portable my VDU my organiser my mouse
oh my filofax my cellnet my daisywheel.

What he dreams driving home at the wheel
on the brimming motorway: her electronics
the green screen of her underwear her digital display.

Oh my spreadsheet he groans in the night:
my modem my cursor lusting after her floppies
wanting her printout her linkup her entire database.

First Echo

I recall the high trees rocking in the wind,
across the road where the soldiers drilled.
They learned their trades there, and went to war.
Beyond was unknown country, fields and distance
where the sun went out.
                    One day my shout
among the tall trees found its echo there,
bouncing my name back among the elms,
calling and calling at the house back
and a second out of time the voice of *not-me*,
repeating all I said though what I said
was only *I, I, I am...*

How does anyone write anything?
How do they begin, in what gesture,
in what moment of prayer, the pen
to the paper? What would anybody say?

Charles Tomlinson *was born in 1927 at Stoke-on-Trent and is a poet, translator, critic and painter. His work has appeared in all major European countries, besides Japan and the USA.*

John Maydew or The Allotment

Ranges
  of clinker heaps
    go orange now:
through cooler air
  an acrid drift
    seeps upwards
from the valley mills;
  the spoiled and staled
    distances invade
these closer comities
  of vegetable shade,
    glass-houses, rows
and trellises of red-
  ly flowering beans.
    This
is a paradise
  where you may smell
    the cinders
of quotidian hell beneath you;
  here grow
    their green reprieves
for those
  who labour, linger in
    their watch-chained waistcoats
rolled-back sleeves —
  the ineradicable

            peasant in the dispossessed
and half-tamed Englishman.
   By day, he makes
      a burrow of necessity
from which,
   at evening, he emerges
      here.
A thoughtful yet unthinking man,
   John Maydew,
      memory stagnates
in you and breeds
   a bitterness; it grew
      and rooted in your silence
from the day
   you came
      unwitting out of war
in all the pride
   of ribbons and a scar
      to forty years
of mean amends...
   He squats
      within his shadow
and a toad
   that takes
      into a slack and twitching jaw
the worms he proffers it,
   looks up at him
      through eyes that are
as dimly faithless
   as the going years.
      For, once returned
he found that he
   must choose between
      an England, profitlessly green
and this —
   a seamed and lunar grey
      where slag in lavafolds
unrolls beneath him.

The valley gazes up
  through kindling eyes
as, unregarded at his back
 its hollows deepen
   with the black, extending shadows
and the sounds of day
  explore its coming cavities,
   the night's
refreshed recesses.
 Tomorrow
  he must feed its will,
his interrupted pastoral
 take heart into
   those close
and gritty certainties that lie
 a glowing ruse
  all washed in hesitations now.
He eyes the toad
 beating
   in the assuagement
of his truce.

Swimming Chenango Lake

Winter will bar the swimmer soon.
 He reads the water's autumnal hesitations
A wealth of ways: it is jarred,
 It is astir already despite its steadiness,
Where the first leaves at the first
 Tremor of the morning air have dropped
Anticipating him, launching their imprints
 Outwards in eccentric, overlapping circles.
There is a geometry of water, for this
 Squares off the clouds' redundances
And sets them floating in a nether atmosphere
 All angles and elongations: every tree
Appears a cypress as it stretches there
 And every bush that shows the season,
A shaft of fire. It is a geometry and not
 A fantasia of distorting forms, but each
Liquid variation answerable to the theme
 It makes away from, plays before:
It is a consistency, the grain of the pulsating flow.
 But he has looked long enough, and now
Body must recall the eye to its dependence
 As he scissors the waterscape apart
And sways it to tatters. Its coldness
 Holding him to itself, he grants the grasp,
For to swim is also to take hold
 On water's meaning, to move in its embrace
And to be, between grasp and grasping, free.
 He reaches in-and-through to that space
The body is heir to, making a where
 In water, a possession to be relinquished
Willingly at each stroke. The image he has torn
 Flows-to behind him, healing itself,
Lifting and lengthening, splayed like the feathers
 Down an immense wing whose darkening spread
Shadows his solitariness: alone, he is unnamed
 By this baptism, where only Chenango bears a name

In a lost language he begins to construe —
 A speech of densities and derisions, of half-
Replies to the questions his body must frame
 Frogwise across the all but penetrable element.
Human, he fronts it and, human, he draws back
 From the interior cold, the mercilessness
That yet shows a kind of mercy sustaining him.
 The last sun of the year is drying his skin
Above a surface a mere mosaic of tiny shatterings,
 Where a wind is unscaping all images in the flowing
 obsidian,
The going-elsewhere of ripples incessantly shaping.

Acknowledgements

Dannie Abse
The Mistake, Breakfast Together and **Two Photographs** from **On the Evening Road**, Hutchinson, 1994.

Fleur Adcock
Post Office and **For Heidi with Blue Hair** from **The Incident Book**, Oxford University Press, 1986, by permission of Oxford University Press.

James Berry
Faces Around My Father and **Spirits of Movement** from **Hot Earth Cold Earth**, Bloodaxe, 1995.

Alan Brownjohn
Profoundest Love, Lieder (For Peter Porter) and **Looking at Her** from **Collected Poems**, Hutchinson, 1988.

Catherine Byron
The Lampshade Makers and **Shears** from **The Fat-Hen Field Hospital**, Loxwood Stoneleigh, 1993.

Wendy Cope
Flowers and **Some More Light Verse** from **Serious Concerns**, Faber and Faber, 1992. **An Attempt At Unrhymed Verse** uncollected: reproduced with the author's permission.

Robert Creeley
Goodbye uncollected: reproduced with the author's permission.

Kwame Dawes
Shadow Play, Oakland Avenue and **Some Tentative Definitions XI** from **Shook Foil** (unpublished): reproduced with the author's permission.

Carol Ann Duffy
Litany, Warming Her Pearls and **Mrs Aesop** from **Selected Poems**, Penguin, 1994.

Helen Dunmore
Yellow, Night Cat and **Breeze of Ghosts**, from **Secrets**, Bodley Head, 1994.
Copyright (c) Helen Dunmore 1994. Reproduced by kind permission of the Author and A P Watt Limited.

Gavin Ewart

Haiku: A Japanese Dried Flower at a Poetry Reading and **Reputations** from **The Complete Little Ones**, Hutchinson, 1986. **The Young Pobble's Guide To His Toes, In the Old People's Home** and **In Memoriam Sir John Betjeman (1906-84)** from **The Young Pobble's Guide To His Toes**, Hutchinson, 1985.

U.A. Fanthorpe

Awkward Subject from **Neck Verse**, Peterloo Poets, 1992. **Dying Fall** from **Safe as Houses**, Peterloo Poets, 1995. Copyright U.A. Fanthorpe, reproduced by permission of Peterloo Poets.

Elaine Feinstein

Dad, Anniversary and **Getting Older**, from **Selected Poems,** Carcanet, 1994.

John Harvey

Seven Year Ache, You Did It! You Did It!, Self Portrait, uncollected, reproduced with the author's permission.

Adrian Henri

The Bell from **Wish You Were Here**, Cape, 1990. **Any Prince to Any Princess** from **Collected Poems**, Allison & Busby, 1986: by permission of the author c/o Rogers, Coleridge & White Ltd., 20 Powys Mews, London W11 1JN. **Love in Blackpool**, uncollected, reproduced with the author's permission.

Selima Hill

Being Fifty Makes me Feel Large from **Violet**, Bloodaxe, 1996. **Silence** from **Trembling Hearts in the Bodies of Dogs**, Bloodaxe, 1994. **Cow** from **A Little Book of Meat**, Bloodaxe, 1993.

Mick Imlah

Goldilocks from **Birthmarks**, Chatto & Windus, 1988.

Jenny Joseph

Uncartography, Piano practice exercises and **Dirge** from **Ghosts and Other Company**, Bloodaxe, 1995.

Jackie Kay

Dance of the Cherry Blossom from **The Adoption Papers**, Bloodaxe, 1991. **The Red Graveyard** from **Other Lovers**, Bloodaxe, 1993. **Sassenachs** from **Two's Company**, Puffin, 1994.

Liz Lochhead
The Redneck from **Penguin Modern Poets 4**, Penguin, 1995.
What The Pool Said, On Midsummer's Day from **Dreaming Frankenstein**, Polygon, 1984.

Michael Longley
Snow Bunting from **The Ghost Orchid**, Cape, 1995. **The Ice-Cream Man**, from **Gorse Fires**, Secker & Warburg, 1991. **Badger**, from **Poems, 1963-1983**, Secker & Warburg, 1991.

John Lucas
Cheers, Arrivals and **News From Nowhere**, uncollected: reproduced with the author's permission.

Roger McGough
Defying Gravity from **Penguin Modern Poets 4**, Penguin, 1995.

Ian McMillan
Kake Yourself Comfortable, Death's Feet and **Dad, the Donkey's on Fire** from **Dad, the Donkey's on Fire**, Carcanet, 1994.

Wes Magee
In the Castle of Gloom and **Our Miss Gill and Mr Scott** uncollected: reproduced with the author's permission.

Adrian Mitchell
Beattie Is Three, Back in the Playground Blues and **Stufferation**, from **Adrian Mitchell's Greatest Hits**, Bloodaxe, 1991.

Henry Normal
The Eating of a Unicorn and **The Frame of the Mona Lisa Dreams**, uncollected: reproduced with the author's permission.

Brian Patten
A Blade of Grass from **Love Poems**, Flamingo, 1994. **The Ambush** from **Storm Damage**, Flamingo, 1995. **The Last Gift** from **Grinning Jack**, Flamingo, 1995.

Tom Paulin
Matins and **Klee/Clover** from **Walking a Line**, Faber, 1994. **A New Society** from **A State of Justice**, Faber, 1977.

Nigel Planer
Assuming you go first and **Rage, rage (against the designing of life)**, unpublished. Reproduced with the author's permission.

Peter Porter
In Rosewell from **The Chair of Babel**, Oxford 1992. **And No Help Came** and **Throw the Book at Them** from **The Automatic Oracle**, Oxford, 1987. **Doll's House** from **Fast Forward**, Oxford, 1984, by permission of Oxford University Press.

Peter Redgrove
At the Edge of the Wood and **Orchard With Wasps** from **Poems, 1954-1987**, Penguin Books, 1989.

Christopher Reid
An Angel and **A Box** from **Katerina Brac,** Faber and Faber, 1985.

Vernon Scannell
A Case of Murder and **Two Variations on an Old Theme** from **Collected Poems, 1950-1993,** Robson Books, 1993.

Penelope Shuttle
Big Cat, Georgette and **My Moon** from **Taxing the Rain**, Oxford University Press, 1992.

Ken Smith
Sunk Island, that winter from **The Poet Reclining** Bloodaxe, 1982. **Yuppy Love** and **First echo** from **the heart, the border,** Bloodaxe, 1990.

Jon Silkin
Harebell and **Death of a Son** from **Selected Poems**, Sinclair-Stevenson, 1994.

Charles Tomlinson
John Maydew or The Allotment and **Swimming Chenango Lake** from **Collected Poems**, Oxford University Press, 1985, by permission of Oxford University Press.

Postscript

How this anthology came about

Of all the roles which the public library fulfils, perhaps the most important one is that of bringing books and readers together. When the opportunity arises to bring readers and writers together, a new dimension is added to the library's work.

It was with the aim of strengthening the library's role in literature promotion that I put on a brief series of poetry readings at Beeston Library in the Spring of 1983, with financial assistance from Nottinghamshire County Council Leisure Services and East Midlands Arts. That first series was an experiment - there had been poetry performances in Nottingham, sponsored by the County Council, but there had never been a sustained series of readings featuring mainstream 'literary' writers.

That first programme featured such names as Dannie Abse, Patricia Beer, Douglas Dunn, Gavin Ewart, Christopher Logue, Peter Porter, Craig Raine, Vernon Scannell and D.M. Thomas. The response was sufficiently encouraging to make a second series feasible, and the reputation of Beeston Library as a venue for poetry performance has gone from strength to strength ever since.

1997 will see the fifteenth series, and this collection has been produced to celebrate fifteen years of memorable evenings at Beeston. It's a 'thank you' to those who have supported the series over the years, a recognition of the many first-rate writers who have performed locally, and, if you have never tried 'Poets in Beeston', a taste of what you have missed!

This anthology contains a representative selection of work from most of the poets who have appeared at Beeston. Thanks are due to the authors and the publishers for permission to reproduce the poems in these pages — a full list of acknowledgements appears elsewhere.

I hope that all lovers of poetry will find much to enjoy among these poems, many of which have never before been published.

Robert Gent

MORE POETRY FROM FIVE LEAVES

THE DYBBUK OF DELIGHT: AN ANTHOLOGY OF JEWISH WOMEN'S POETRY
Edited by Sonja Lyndon and Sylvia Paskin
236 pages, £9.99, flapped paperback, 0 907123 57 0
A major celebration of Jewish women's creativity, covering the interests of contemporary Jewish women, religious and secular. 62 contributors including Elaine Feinstein, Ruth Fainlight, Rabbi Elizabeth Sarah, Michelene Wandor, Wanda Barford, Lotte Kramer, Valerie Sinason and Sue Hubbard.

The Dybbuk of Delight is a remarkable collection of poems: passionate, witty, often heartbreaking.
Ham and High

THE SKIN OF YOUR BACK
Michael Rosen
64 pages, £5.50, paperback, 0 907123 66 X
A book of poems ranging over politics, sex, disturbing encounters and satires. Michael Rosen draws on experiences as diverse as cremations, milk fever, anatomy lessons and the war in Bosnia. The poems are provocative, thoughtful and occasionally wistful as they wind around some old haunts of left wing politics and bizarre individuals. Committed, sexy, Jewish, funny, punchy.

YOU ARE, AREN'T YOU?
Michael Rosen
72 pages, £4.99, paperback, 0 907123 09 0
A collection of Jewish and socialist poems. Michael Rosen's first book of poems for an adult audience.

LAUGHING ALL THE WAY
Liz Cashdan
72 pages, £5.99, paperback, 0 907123 46 5
Liz Cashdan's poems convey a strong sense of personal identity and include the acclaimed Tyre-Cairo letters, a dramatic reconstruction of the life of an 11th century Jewish family.

NEW FROM FIVE LEAVES

THE SLOW MIRROR AND OTHER STORIES: NEW FICTION BY JEWISH WRITERS
Edited by Sonja Lyndon and Sylvia Paskin
240 pages, £8.99, paperback, 0 907123 81 3
An anthology of new short stories by Jewish writers from Britain, the USA and South Africa. In styles ranging from magical realism to erotic fantasy, from the reality of everyday life to wicked humour, this collection reflects modern Jewish life and concerns.
The 23 contributors include Elaine Feinstein, Ellen Galford, Jack Gratus, Dan Jacobson, Gabriel Josipovici, Frederic Raphael, Michelene Wandor, Shelley Weiner, Jonathan Wilson and Richard Zimler.

THE SHALLOW GRAVE: A MEMOIR OF THE SPANISH CIVIL WAR
Walter Gregory
188 pages, £6.99, paperback, 0 907123 61 9
A remarkable memoir by a member of the International Brigade who fought in all of the major battles of the Civil War. Walter Gregory was wounded three times and captured on the last day the British Battalion fought. He was sentenced to death by Franco's forces, but was eventually released.

To read Walter Gregory's memoir is to breathe again the heady air of myth and belief... and to know that for the generation of the 1930s, their Spanish Civil War will never end.
Daily Telegraph

All books published by Five Leaves are available from bookshops or, post-free from Five Leaves Publications, PO Box 81, Nottingham, NG5 4ER. Trade orders UK/Europe — Central Books, USA/Canada — AK Press.